WORKING WITH
COLOR

WORKING WITH
COLOR

A MANUAL FOR PAINTERS

Irving Kriesberg

Prentice Hall Press · New York

Special thanks to Bruce Barton for the black-and-white drawings. His clear understanding of the issues makes him much more than a good graphic artist. Special thanks, also, to editor David Sachs, whose active enthusiasm is responsible for much that is good in this book.

Published by Prentice Hall Press
A Division of Simon & Schuster, Inc.

PRENTICE HALL PRESS is a trademark of Simon & Schuster, Inc.

Library of Congress Cataloging in Publication Data

Kriesberg, Irving, 1919-
    Working with color.

    Includes index.
    1. Color in art.   2. Color—Psychological aspects.
3. Artists' studios.   I. Title.
ND1488.K75   1985   752   84-7573

ISBN: 0-671-60729-4

Manufactured in the United States of America.

    2 3 4 5 6 7 8 9 10

CONTENTS

We think in order to act;
Act in order to think.

—Goethe

INTRODUCTION

Although color is only one of a complex of elements that go into the construction of a painting, it is an extremely important element, and over the past 100 years it has played an increasingly critical role in works of any style. Color in painting can also be a very elusive subject, not easily harnessed by speech and writing. Perhaps for this very reason—that it is an important and difficult subject for painters—we should attempt to explore it thoroughly. To do so, we must use our mind and eye as precisely and as exhaustively as we can, focusing very closely. At the same time, we must maintain a long-range view, bearing in mind the intricately balanced ecology of each of the works we examine.

For the painter, there is no such thing as color theory; there are no prescriptions. The most useful classroom courses in color consist essentially of a series of exercises designed to train the eye to more precise perception, generally by trying out all sorts of juxtapositions. Exercises can also give students more controlled experience in mixing paints, so they can more easily anticipate how one pigment will react when combined with another.

Scientific theories of color as light are irrelevant to the artist's concerns, as are researches into the physiology of color perception. All the various formats for color wheels supposedly based on the spectrum of sunlight have no relevant authority: it is useful for the beginner to paint color wheels because that experience trains the eye to judge color differences more precisely, but color wheels in themselves prove nothing and yield no formulas to help the painter create a successful painting.

Some writers also offer lists of personal color associations, which they try to pass off as principles of color. These lists usually boil down to saying that purple is somber, red is exciting, yellow is happy, and so forth. Such associations are hardly universal, however: to many Buddhists, for example, yellow symbolizes holiness, and in many cultures of the world white is the color of mourning. Anyone who talks about blue as purity or red as danger is talking about signs, not about art.

I myself have no consolidated theory of color to propound, and I know of none that has general efficacy.

We can only affirm that art is unpredictable and magical. The marvelous thing about painting is that the bit of green paint lifted from your palette and spread upon the canvas remains a patch of paint to our mind's eye, but becomes also a leaf, a hollow, conveys calm or builds toward climax, rests heavy in our bones or sends us flying. The magic that makes this possible is the magic of the human mind. I don't propose to talk about that mystery—only about the craft and awareness of the magician-painter: what it is the painter does to bring that wonder to the beholder's eye.

*   *   *

Early in the last century, William Hazlitt recorded the story of how a much-admired watercolor of a harbor scene by Turner gained its arresting red buoy.

It seems that the managers of the Royal British Academy had, for its annual exhibition, accepted a painting by Constable and one by Turner, which were to hang side by side. The Constable was a large, heavily impastoed canvas, while the Turner was a modest, mild watercolor. When Turner learned of the intended hanging arrangement, he objected that his small, slight painting would inevitably be swamped by the large Constable, but the trustees would not hear him.

On varnishing day (the day before the exhibition's opening, when all the invited artists were expected to give their paintings a final inspection and a final coat of varnish), Turner appeared with his box of watercolors. Gazing at his painting—and no doubt enraged—he dipped his brush into the moist red on his palette and quickly painted a bright red buoy in the midst of his calm scene. The red rang like a buzzer, riveting attention to the small painting—at the expense of the heavy oil just next to it.

Now, does this little tale illustrate the power of an appropriate spot of color to transform a work—or does it illustrate the power of emotion, a single flush of anger?

The answer, fairly obviously, is both—inseparably. From this follows my real point: that however much we analyze and talk about composition and color strategies and any other aspect of a finished work, we are talking about only part of the creative act.

*   *   *

If you are taking up this book in order to improve your own painting, it is important that you do more than simply read it. Going through this book without engaging in the exercises is much like reading a book about diet or fitness without taking any action. The mind and eye need exercise as much as do the legs or the torso.

The second important thing to be said about the exercises is that they are just that. The little structures and devices you will paint in response to the exercise instructions are not in themselves works of art. Real paintings come into existence while the artist is not consciously thinking about rules and principles, just as—in the art of dance—the true dancer is not thinking about the steps to be executed during a performance, but is moved by emotion. Yet surely the dancer could not perform superbly without having very consciously developed a disciplined and capable body by means of exercises.

My advice, then, is that you do these exercises. Do them precisely, without thinking of aesthetics. Then later, on another canvas, when you make a painting, do not think of the exercises.

Just as doing color exercises helps train the eye in subtle optical differences, so the discussion of aesthetics can train the artist's mind. This training serves not so much to determine what is good or bad, but to determine more precisely your own intentions. One artist may want to express a softly resonant quality;

another, something strident and brusque. One may choose a palette with a quiet range of colors; another may want to juggle a wide array of contrasting colors. One may be seeking to render the atmospheric effects of deep space; another may seek to suggest deep space by contrasting areas of flat color. All these qualities and a million more are possible, and all are legitimate. The appropriateness of a color or group of colors or of a mode of application is always related to the artist's particular intention in making the painting.

That is the only principle I can justly state; the rest is observation.

PART 1

TASTING
COLOR

*Exercising Your
Aesthetic Taste Buds*

Pablo Picasso *The Studio*. Oil on canvas, 1928 (59 x 91 inches). Collection, The Museum of Modern Art, New York. Gift of Walter P. Chrysler, Jr.

1
HUE

In painting there are many ways to designate a patch of color. We start
with hue, but we end with function.

We are so accustomed to speaking of color in terms of hue only—red, yellow,
green, and so on—that we tend to forget how many qualities we might perceive
in a given patch of red or yellow or green. Not only are a thousand tones of each
hue possible, but other factors besides hue contribute to our total perception of
the patch of color: qualities such as brightness, coolness, resonance, tactility,
directness; contextual functions such as a variation, a shift, a climax. The fact that
many of these characteristics can be called subjective and that no two people will
agree on all the terms with which to describe the patch of color in no way robs it
of such properties.

This first chapter, therefore, is devoted to an inventory of the qualities we
might observe in some of the patches found in the paintings reproduced in this
book.* Let us here focus on the color red.

The last works of Mondrian, collectively called *Boogie Woogie*, are complex
pathways and stations of color which chug along rhythmically. Our reproduction shows a portion of the unfinished *Victory Boogie Woogie*. Before applying the

*This is an appropriate moment to make a very important caveat about the reproductions in this
book, splendid though I think they are. No printed picture can hope to capture all of the nuances
and impact of the original. The great reduction in size distorts our perception, and each of the
several processes of photography, color separation, and printing contributes its own tiny alteration
of the original. In addition, in order to focus on a particular set of paint qualities, I have occasionally
reproduced here oi.ly a portion of an original painting, thus creating another sort of distortion.

final patches of paint, with their clean straight edges, the artist tried out different colors and sizes by pasting colored tapes or bits of paper to the canvas. Some of these remain on this painting-in-progress; the fact that they are sometimes roughly torn and are now faded or decayed in tone provides a much more varied pulse than we are accustomed to see in a Mondrian.

Nevertheless the familiar staccato of red, blue, yellow, and gray is there. Examining the reds in the paintings reproduced in this book, we find perhaps the purest, most abstract red in the Mondrian. If *Victory Boogie Woogie*'s red squares seem absolute and pure in hue, however, it is not simply because the artist has touched the correct chromatic button. It is the spareness of context, the presence of only strongly contrasting colors such as yellow and blue, that causes us to perceive the squares of red as an example of hue in its most pristine, most nearly absolute state.

The Frank Stella painting *Tahkt-I-Sulayman Variation 1* also consists of seemingly pure colors. Again, the quality of purity or absoluteness is due to a certain greatly reduced context. Within each band there is no modulation of color, and each is isolated by a narrow white border, so that our perception is clear of the complexities that occur when one color abuts another; our eye is free to sample and savor each color in isolation. The importance of context is evinced by the following little experiment: compare the Stella with the painting *Compact Elegance* by Cham Hendon. The two are about as different in concept and feeling as two paintings can be. The Stella is majestic in its elegance; the Hendon wears the label "Elegance" ironically. Yet as you look closely and attempt to match color for color in the two paintings, it is surprising how often and how very nearly you can do so. What can this mean? Evidently, a particular hue in itself conveys very little; our perception requires some context to give meaning and feeling to any spot of color.

As for hue itself, how many of Stella's colors would you categorize as red? Ask your friends to do the same, and see if they come up with the same answers. In contrast to Stella's, Hendon's reds are unabashed, and he sometimes throws them at us so thickly we almost suffocate.

Directing our attention to more traditional modes of painting, it is useful to compare the red of Matthiasdottir's garden-pepper in *Still Life with Cheese and Pepper* and the red of Dufy's roofs across the water in *Open Window, Nice*. The red of the pepper seems inseparable from our perception of the solidity of the object itself; despite its unique color in the painting, we perceive the pepper as one of several hard, separate objects in the picture. Quite different is Dufy's use of red: the dabs that depict the roofs and the pattern on the sofa always come to our eye equally if not primarily as brush strokes, and we can never lose that double awareness.

The red of Picasso's tablecloth in *The Studio* is neither as immaterial as Mondrian's red nor as palpable as Matthiasdottir's. Again, it is not the particular chroma that makes the difference, but the context. Mondrian's red is one beat of an ongoing rhythm, and as such it has a certain specifically abstract or sensate reference. In the Picasso, even if we did not know the title, we would recognize that the red plays a role in some dramatic, almost theatrical arrangement: with its green center, it is a focal point in a drama in which all the other elements are equally involved.

DeKooning's red in *Asheville* is cheery and fleshy. It may also be described as sensate or hedonistic—qualities less central to the Picasso—but it has an emotionality and actuality that the Mondrian does not possess.

Asheville's red emerges out of the several luscious pinks, yellows, and light blues alternately appearing and disappearing behind a veil of white tones and black lines. Near the center of the painting, it flashes brightly, as though the final gesture of an erotic dance.

Consider next the red parasol in Monet's *Parisians Enjoying the Parc Monceau*. The red is at once dusky and bright. Within the portion of the painting reproduced in this book, the red is probably the richest, most saturated spot of color. Yet to understand or to savor the real quality of this red, we need to understand its function in the painting. Starting with the man seated in deep shadow at the extreme right, we can follow the pageant of figures that are seated and standing along the shady path. As our eye moves across the bench of dappled women, we are already aware of a bright pink parasol in distant sunlight, belonging to another party of strollers.

The woman with the red parasol marks a point of mergence between the foreground path in shadow and the sunlit path farther away. She stands in the center of the little group that identifies a gentle area of climax where the two groups of strollers mingle. Meanwhile, we have become aware of the bright sunlight that shows white behind the dark trees (partially cropped in our reproduction) and that shows pink as it splashes on the distant building and on the gardens behind the silhouetted figures.

The woman with the red parasol, then, stands at the convergence of the two paths of strollers and of the plunge of pink light beyond. Her silhouette, like those of her neighbors and of the trees immediately around them, engages the white and pink sunlight, forging links between the shaded lower (or nearer) part of the picture and the sunlit portions above. The surest link of all, though, is the little translucent red of the parasol, which, like some magical prism, gathers the vast whiteness funneled by the tall dark trees and receives the splash of sunlight, filtering it through red, diffusing it, and sending its half-tones to glimmer among the shaded figures and mottled path below.

In itself, the patch of mottled red is not spectacular. Indeed, when the patch is isolated, how are we to describe it: as rich? as bright? as dusky? It is hardly useful to designate a color with a simple word or two. When we speak about color in a painting, we must discuss its function if we are to say anything about it at all.

Much of what follows in this book consists of just such close examinations of the way color functions to build a painting. Clearly, the question is not whether the artist consciously planned these strategies: we can never know that. The most useful thing we can do is to try to ascertain the key factors that determine the coherence we all recognize when we look at a successful work of art.

Claude Monet *Parisians Enjoying the Parc Monceau.* Oil on canvas, 1878
(28⅝ × 21⅜ inches). The Metropolitan Museum of Art, Mr. and Mrs. Henry
Ittleson, Jr., Fund, 1959.

Exercises

1. Choose a color such as blue or green, and see how many examples of that color you can find among the color reproductions. Don't stop at the obvious examples; go to the borderline cases, and then see whether your categorizations match those of your friends.

2. Go over your list of a dozen blues or greens and find your own words to describe them. Go beyond objective words (dark, bright, light) to words that are more arguable (sweet, exhilarating, gritty, smooth) and to words that express the possible role of the color in the painting (unique, climactic, variation, opposition). Again, it will be helpful to compare your answers with those of a friend.

3a. Paint a simple color wheel of six hues: red, orange, yellow, green, blue, violet. Two principles should guide your building of the "correct" red, blue, and so forth: make each of the colors as intense as the others; and let the contrast between each color be equal. Viewed from a distance, none of your six wedges should provide a jump or gap; each color should be a distinct step, and each step should be as nearly equal as you can make it.*

3b. Paint a color wheel containing twelve wedges or segments.

In these and in all succeeding exercises, it is important that you use paint to make the diagrams and constructs. Using colored papers involves you in a

*In the black-and-white drawings of the color wheels, I have indicated different hues with different patterns of lines. I have deliberately kept all the wedges close in value—an equal gray—to indicate that though each wedge in your wheel will be of a different hue, the other characteristics, such as saturation (brightness) and value (degree of dark or light) should be kept as nearly equal as possible for all wedges. For example, you will have to negotiate with your paints to get a violet that is not too much darker than the yellow but at the same time preserves its purity of hue, just as you will have to negotiate a yellow that is dark enough or has enough impact while maintaining its proper yellow hue. Even though these judgments are ultimately subjective, you should have a clear notion of what you are after as you juggle one color against another.

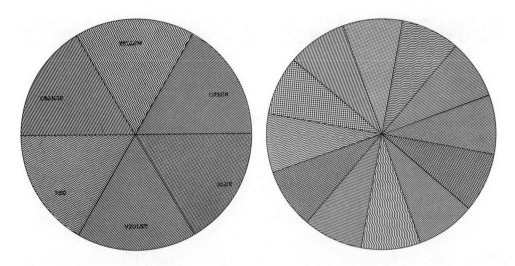

process of choosing among available tones; and no matter how intricate that process may be, it does not afford you the experience of mixing paint, which is a crucial aspect of all the exercises in this book.

Remember, it is not enough that you read these exercises and tell yourself that you understand the issue. It is essential that you go through the painstaking business of mixing colors to get the exact tone you need and of making slight changes in adjacent squares in order to establish the whole relationship.

2
TENSION

You can try for simple balance by repeating colors in different parts of the canvas, but you can also set colors in opposition to each other and thereby achieve a dynamic equilibrium.

In painting it is often useful to think of the canvas as a field held in tension by the force of color. The idea of tension is best illustrated by thinking of a rubber band. When we pick it up, it is limp. When we stretch it—that is, when we pull it in two opposing directions—it becomes tense and alive. In a similar way you can hold out your arm limply or, by bringing into play the arm's system of opposing muscles, make it quiver with tension.

In a characteristic Mondrian, a square of red in the upper left portion of the canvas pulls the eye to that corner of the painting, while a square of blue (somewhat less intense, but a bit larger) exerts an equal pull diagonally opposite. At the same time, a smaller square of intense yellow pulls our eye across the other diagonal. Held flat by the black bands, these pulls make us feel as though our eye were stretched taut across the canvas.

Victory Boogie Woogie, one of Mondrian's last paintings (left unfinished), contains many such squares. As in several of his last paintings, many of the smaller squares are arranged in bands, and our eye tends to march rather than stretch across the canvas. While of course the whole canvas must be seen to enjoy the full play of this very complex work, you can try masking portions of the reproduction so that you see only a few squares at a time.

You will quickly find yourself responding to the tug of individual colors

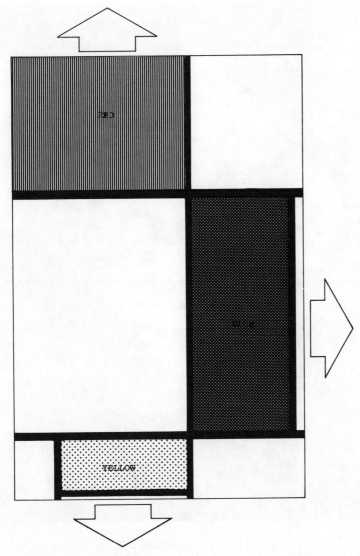

2-1. A schematic rendition of Mondrian's
Composition with Yellow and Blue, 1928.

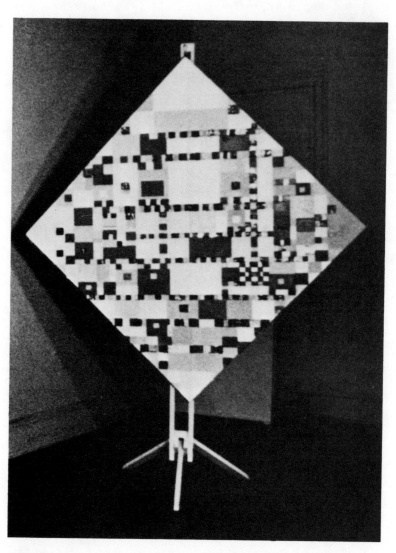

Piet Mondrian *Victory Boogie Woogie*. Oil and tape on canvas, 1944 (unfinished) (50 × 50 inches). Collection, Mr. and Mrs. Burton Tremaine.

much as you respond to the beat of music. When you view a larger portion of the painting, the tension or tautness across the surface of the canvas continues to be evident. Although your eye jumps along the paths, it is also constantly being stretched laterally across the whole face of the canvas. The liveliness of the painting surely derives as much from this tension as it does from the snaking of the red and yellow mosaics.

Pablo Picasso's *The Studio* demonstrates another kind of spatial tension. Despite the title, we realize that the physicality offered by this painting is not that of the solid objects presented to us by the still life of Matthiasdottir. In the Picasso there seems to be a play of elements that are neither solid nor weightless. All elements have a certain equal flatness, yet we perceive the space of a room. Our awareness hovers on the edge between comprehending the elements as abstract areas of color, without specific density or depth, and perceiving them as table, bowl, pictures, and so on. This state of affairs is paradoxical; yet a moment's reflection causes us to realize that all painting contains this paradox. We regularly see representations of the three-dimensional world on a flat surface and representations on a static surface of the flow and shift of emotions, and we accept the paradox, just as we do when at the cinema we sit in our seat for ten minutes and watch ten years roll by.

Really, we can define art precisely in terms of such dual perceptions—perceptions held in tension—and this definition ought to be kept in mind as we examine the Picasso more closely.

The left one-third of the painting is a yellow rectangle representing the painter and his canvas, and the remaining two-thirds is a square representing the studio. The first question we might ask in assessing the total painting is: how is the yellow rectangle brought into relationship with all the other elements?

Initially we see it standing in opposition to them—the large expanse of clear warm color contrasts sharply with the more varied and starkly colored areas on the right. Soon, however, we are aware that the two worlds are locked together by more than the short diagonal line that represents the artist's brush. First we are pulled outward by the border of deeper yellow; then we realize that the two areas are given equal weight by the small but very intense contrast of red and green in the still life, which roughly balances the impact of the rich yellow. Meanwhile, the movement initiated by the expanding yellow frame spreads rightward across the face of the canvas in the form of picture frames marching along the wall and leading to the bust, which is part of the still life and in turn echoes the head of the painter.

Thus a precarious parity is established between left and right, just as an equilibrium is maintained between our perceptions of depth and of flatness; and a final tension is generated by our simultaneous awareness of both abstraction and reality.

Returning to the more physical aspect of tension, I want to make a distinction between tension and balance by defining tension as a system of living equilibrium. I have offered the example of a stretched rubber band; now think of a merchant's simple weighing scales—two pans suspended from a pivoting bar. A large bunch of grapes in one pan is balanced by a small disc of brass in the other, each responding equally to the pull of gravity. The equilibrium of the scales is never passive: it always exhibits a form of tension.

For painters this translates into the fact that most of us don't want to balance grapes with grapes or brass with brass, but that we find delight in constantly weighing out disparate elements. A tension is generated in the process that, in the successful work, holds the entire canvas taut.

The working artist knows that balance alone will not create a sense of living tension: this interplay must be felt as part of the act of painting. The best practical advice I can give is that you look constantly at the whole canvas, so that while you make a mark on the upper right of the canvas, your eye is on the lower left. That unremitting awareness of the total canvas is the source of the tension I am talking about. The pink flower you paint should not only complete your depiction of the bouquet; it should also cause the green table along the bottom of the picture to resonate, to quiver with tension.

Elizabeth Murray's construction *Back on Earth* owes its coherence to pure tension—in this case, a system of oppositions. Her work is large and physically complex. There is, first of all, her opposition of the painted patterns to the patterns of the cutout contours. In addition, the two-color patterns may be said to exist in opposition to each other: the pair of greens versus the blue and black. While the right-hand section is devoted to the pattern of greens and the left-hand section to blue and black, the division is not really so clear-cut; and the more we look, the more exceptions we see.

The complex play of elements is consequently never resolved—or rather, never brought to rest. The pattern of the cutout both responds to and opposes the painted pattern: one of the painted series of shapes, the black, is so nearly absolute in its color and so vigorous in its design that it rivals the actuality of the cutout. Besides, so many links and correspondences exist between the paint and the cutout that we are never sure they are quite in opposition. It is as if one of a pair of magnets were kept rotating, creating a continuous pattern of attraction and repulsion.

This is the source of the dynamism which so activates this energetic piece, keeping it always both raw and coherent. The clear articulation of a paradox gives the object an undeniable wholeness, as well as tension.

Some people may contend that *Back on Earth* is a hybrid piece—part painting, part sculpture, and never completely either. Murray herself, however, presents the quandary with so lively a frankness that theoretical objections melt before they can be stated. Alternatively, we can say that this entire issue is one more aspect of the series of tensions the work exhibits.

Exercises

1. Mark off six rectangles, 8″ × 10″ each. Fill each rectangle with a different color. Then paint a disc of contrasting color in the upper left corner of each. Then, in the lower right corner, paint an element that, by its color, extent, or configuration, will provide a balance to the first image.

Prepare six new rectangles and do the same, this time using three elements

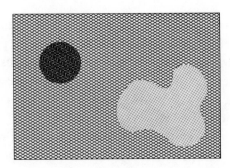

2. Make a 7″ × 9″ rectangle of a single color. Paint a jagged line of some other color across the rectangle's face. The resulting two areas of color must be active enough along the jagged edge that both portions of the rectangle appear "positive"—as if each had been painted around that jagged line. From the passive single block of color, you should have created a rectangle containing two active parts.

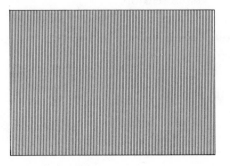 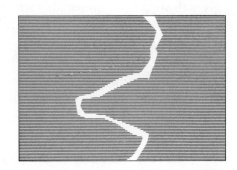

3. On a single sheet, paint a dozen simple but different silhouette images; give each equal impact. If, for example you paint a bunch of purple grapes, a brass weight, a red hand, and nine other images, you will have to balance out their size, brightness of color, complexity of contour, and so forth, so that each of the twelve silhouettes has approximately equal impact on the sheet of paper.

3
___

MOVEMENT

Most artists want their works to be dynamic rather than static. Vitality depends upon generating movement.

As must already be clear, I do not believe that a patch of red in one corner of a painting necessarily needs to be repeated somewhere else on the canvas, or that a spot of blue here calls for a bit of blue there. I think this sort of repetition creates not balance, but boredom.

It is far more interesting to generate a sense in the viewer of moving through the canvas from one situation to another, from one condition to another. Such an effect allows us to feel that we are going from clear, refreshing tones here to more dense and resonant tones there.

The Frank Stella painting *Tahkt* is a good example of a work that avoids simple decorative spotting of color. The painting is divided into completely separate areas of color—perhaps one and a half dozen of them, counting bands and spaces—and none of the colors is repeated. Moreover, the theme of the format is certainly repetition; so it is chiefly by the skillful management of his color that the artist has achieved the vitality his work so abundantly radiates.

The most striking group of contrasts occurs at the extreme right with the combination of black, peach-yellow, and deep red. Leftward we move through an area of relative calm until we reach the strong russet red protractor, which continues the leftward movement to the place at which the rich rose colors combine with the strong green and deep blue to generate a pull that, though more diffused, is as strong as the sharp pull of red and black at the other end.

Traditionally, movement in a painting has been most often effected by the judicious placement of forms in space, so that our eye, moving from one mass to another, is led through the spatial area depicted. In looking at the figures that occupy the foreground space of Monet's painting, our eye moves from right to left as it scans the seated forms along the shady path. Among the devices by which our eye is led horizontally is the placement of the two small children playing at their mothers' knees. Their precise location has the effect of stretching the women's laps, affirming the horizontally of the path; at the same time, the forms of the children are in themselves essentially vertical, so they constitute a beginning of the verticality that is affirmed farther on by the standing figures and still later by the pattern of the foliage that dominates the upper portion of the painting.

Despite the seemingly spontaneous play of brush strokes, these forms are quite apparent to our eye and the flow of movement they generate is firm and hardly equivocal.

Many early twentieth century paintings exhibit such spatial management in a more complex or problematic manner. Matisse's *Interior with Etruscan Vase* is a good example, for it is a painting that at first seems static, and then, as we examine it more closely, becomes astonishingly dynamic.

The seeming symmetry of the painting is established by the frontal position of the woman who is very much in the center of the picture—a very difficult premise from which to generate an active composition. The centrality of the woman is strengthened by the mirror behind her, which reaches up to the top of the painting, and by the ends of her gown, which reconstruct the rectangle of the mirror and draw it down almost to the bottom of the painting. Further, we see that this vertical rectangle is set within the horizontal rectangle of the table.

The features described thus far point to an insistent and static centrality; but then we notice that the table is really moved over considerably to the left, generating closeness on the left and openness on the right. The right is less crowded not only from east to west, but also from north to south, for we are given plenty of floor space on that side before the intervention of the large vase standing on its light blue platform. Thus a diagonal is created from lower left to middle right. Almost as soon as we are aware of the light blue base, we become aware of the leaning pitcher, which sends our eye up along a sharp diagonal to be caught and spread by the set of little pictures at the upper left.

These diagonals break up the frontality of the design by their contrasting directions and also generate a sense of depth, since diagonals in painting are usually read by the eye as an indication of perspective.

Nevertheless, notice that the group of little pictures, while helping establish a strong diagonal, occurs in a space that vertically lines up with the left edge of the table legs. The legs are in the very foreground of the picture space and the drawings are on the back wall, so we become aware that those light grey squares are producing two conflicting results at once: they help establish both a diagonal and a vertical, and thus they help establish both depth and flatness.

This play of paradox is evident in the way the strongly patterned curtain on the left hugs the front left edge of the painting, while at the same time offering itself as a clear balance to the large vase standing in open space halfway back in the room; and the paradoxical relationship is established not only by the shape and relation of the two entities, but by their color as well. Against so much black and green in the painting, the red curtain and the orange vase would seem to constitute a pair. Yet the linear red of the curtain belongs just as much to the striped robe of the woman, and the orange vase belongs just as much to her face and to the other warm-colored pots and fruits scattered along a wide horizontal path in the painting, as the two do to each other.

The casualness of the foliage, left and right, also evidences this play of symmetry versus dynamism. On the right, in the supposedly more open portion of the picture space, the green leaves are relatively bunched up and—despite their riotous contours—are restricted to the upper right square of the picture, whereas the other group of leaves, belonging to the smallish pot on the table, straddles with its extending fronds a very substantial and open amount of picture space.

The dark green of the plant leaves, at first hardly distinguishable from the blackish background, provides a surprising airiness and spatiality, as against the scatter of bright-colored objects that serves to establish a flatter, horizontal-vertical dispersion.

Many elements besides color contribute to the dynamism of this painting—line, shape, and interval, for example—but if we were to look at a black and white reproduction of this work, very little of what we have been talking about would be evident.

Like the Matisse, Helen Frankenthaler's *Aries* presents itself as a quite spontaneous work. *Aries*, however, is not built so firmly on an architectural framework as is the Matisse, even though its huge splashes clearly make us aware of the canvas's center and of their relation to the perimeter; nor does the painting offer such a clear path of movement for the eye. Indeed, our eye is not offered movement so much as juxtapositions, as if the mind were presented with a series of alternatives rather than with unequivocal structures.

The firm bands of deep yellow and bright blue along the top seem to anchor the composition to that edge of the canvas. Along the bottom, the same yellow combines with a rich red to play a similar if less certain role. In the center, the horizontal meeting of mild green and diluted red constitute a tentative echo of that geometry. Toward the left, though, the abrupt diagonal of light green and the altogether eccentric forms of white (the raw canvas) seriously disrupt any symmetry of pattern. We become increasingly aware of the arbitrary quality of the splashes of watery paint—which are even more apparent in the large original—so that in the end it becomes difficult to speak of a single unquestionable movement or balance to which the painting's coherence may be ascribed.

Even less susceptible to structural analysis is Willem de Kooning's painting *Asheville*, which strikes us at first as a chaotic jumble of lines and colors. Although we detect fragments of architectural and organic forms, it seems impossible ever to organize the space into the firm, unequivocal forms of the Matisse.

Yes, we can note the exceptional square of light green on the left and the large eyelike black form on the right, and we can speak of some rudimentary balance; but surely that is not an essential quality of the work. We do feel, nonetheless, a persistent sense of cohesiveness as well as a definite sense of center. Contributing strongly to the sense of center are the colors that are brightest and most sharply juxtaposed in the middle area. In this reading, the composition might be called a sort of rectangular solar system, with the centrifugal (outgoing) pulls matched by the centripetal (inward gravitational) force, and with the whole kept moving by active tension.

The last statement above still represents an attempt to see a single overall composition. The noted art critic Harold Rosenberg argued against such attempts in looking at de Kooning's work of this period (circa 1950) and—in a luminous piece of writing, as poetic as it is theoretical—he describes the sense of these paintings.

> The Surrealists had been content to handle their dream creations as if they were natural objects: . . . they were, in respect to painting, things no different from ordinary pianos or birds. . . . De Kooning, on the other hand . . . has said "the idea of space is given to the artist to change if he can. . . ." De Kooning releases the shape that is both an abstract sign and the emblem of a concrete experience from the stasis of objects located in deep space in order to make it function in a new kind of psychodynamic composition. Produced by gesture, as in writing, but differing from calligraphy in preserving the sense of solidity characteristic of traditional Western art, each of his forms is engaged as a separate integer of suggestion in a complex interaction at once formal and subjective. . . . The figurations of de Kooning come into being through inspired flaunts of the brush, sideswipe the mind in passing from one into another with a continuous effect on meaning grasped then lost.*

These observations are general and address themselves more to an aesthetic position than to the particular elements of a given painting. Sometimes, however, that is the more fruitful way to go. Elsewhere in this book, I refer to specific qualities of *Asheville*; but in the matter of movement, we must conclude that any general plan is "elusive" and indeed that it might be better to speak of the painting's changefulness, rather than of its pattern of movement.

*Harold Rosenberg, *De Kooning* (New York: Harry Abrams, 1974), p. 21.

Exercises

1a. Divide a long horizontal space, 3″ × 10″, into twelve vertical bands, each a different color; you may repeat some of the colors or not, as you wish. Arrange the colors so that an essentially static balance is achieved among the twelve bands.

1b. Paint another set of twelve adjacent bands with a selection of colors that, to your eye, generates movement from left to right.

2. This time, paint two sets of twelve bands, one resting exactly on top of the other. Arrange your twenty-four colors to generate a zigzag or up-and-down movement from left to right.

3. Finally, paint a single series of fourteen bands. Try to generate a sense of in-and-out or alternate protrusion and retraction as your eye moves from left to right.

Cham Hendon, *Compact Elegance*. Acrylic on canvas, 1981 (32¾ × 51 inches).
(Courtesy, Phyllis Kind, New York.)

Frank Stella, *Tahkt-I-Sulayman Variation 1*. Polymer and fluorescent polymer on canvas,
1969 (120 × 240 inches). (Courtesy, Leo Castelli Gallery, New York.)

Louisa Matthiasdottir, *Still Life with Cheese and Pepper*. Oil on canvas, 1978 (21 × 22 inches). (Private Collection: Courtesy Robert Schoelkopf Gallery, Ltd., N.Y. Courtesy, The Robert Schoelkopf Gallery, New York.)

Philip Guston, *Untitled*. Acrylic on paper, 1980 (23 × 29 inches). (Courtesy, David McKee, New York.)

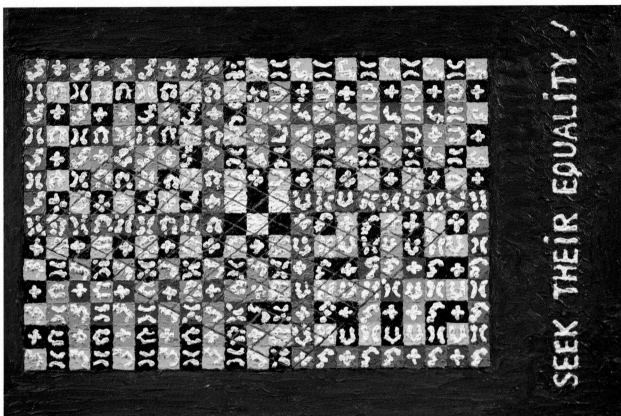

Alfred Jensen, *Equality III Seek Their Equality*. Oil on canvas, 1972 (42 × 28 inches). (Courtesy, The Pace Gallery, New York.)

Irving Kriesberg, *Portrait of Leo Steinberg* (detail). Oil on canvas, 1981 (34 × 28 inches). (Courtesy of the artist.)

Elizabeth Murray, *Back on Earth*. Oil on canvas, 1981 (120½ × 135 inches).
(Collection, Art Institute of Chicago.)

4

SCALE

> It is important that color progressions and oppositions be kept to a
> consistent scale. It is dangerous to walk a stairway whose steps are of
> different heights.

In art, the word "scale" often refers to the size or scope of a work; but for present
purposes we need to remember that the word is related to the Italian *scala*, which
refers to a stairway or ladder or more generally to any system of steps or
increments. You know how difficult and even dangerous it is to walk a stairway
whose steps are of uneven height. On the other hand, we can feel secure, even in
the dark, if we know that the next step will be at a predictable distance from the
one we are on.

In a given painting, our eye may move from one color to another, or even
jump from one very different color to another, and do so with a sense of security
if the artist has maintained a consistent scale—if the artist's steps, tiny or great,
have a given regularity. A common error of beginners, in painting a portrait, for
example, is to make the shirt one bright color and the background another,
contrasting strong color, only to modulate the colors of the face carefully with
only slight shifts of color. Thus the scale of steps in one part of the canvas is not
consistent with that in another part. In such a case it is not simply the scale that
has shifted, but the language of the painting itself—the terms by which the canvas
is read. The result is confused or uncertain legibility.

Another way to describe scale is in terms of consistency of articulation.
When we watch a dancer, we enjoy the clarity of movement of the dancer's
limbs; every shift or turn of a knee, an elbow, a wrist, adds to the precision of
expression. If an arm is flung abruptly, the action conveys one meaning; if it is

flung gently, it conveys another. A comparable situation exists with painting and the application of color. You may choose to construct your canvas with large areas of bold color or you may choose to build with tiny increments of hue.

To carry the analogy of the dancer further: in how many ways can a wrist be moved? Left; right; up; back; forward; abruptly; smoothly; in short, in as many ways as the dancer's imagination and skill will allow. A movement always proceeds from one situation to another. Now, color moves also. It proceeds from red to pink, from light to dark, from bright to dull, from warm to cool, from thick to thin, from sweet to acid, from strident to suave, and so on indefinitely, limited only by the artist's richness of imagination and clarity of intentions. Suppose, for example, that you are painting the image of a flower. You may choose to load your brush with dark green, proceed upward along the canvas with a few branching strokes, add at the top a knot of blue, and then splash some brilliant red as the petaled flower. That brusqueness is one sort of articulation and may be what you want. Alternatively, you may lean toward a more modulated expression in which each leaf and portion of stem is constructed of quiet shifts, a light warm (yellowish) green giving way to a cool whitish green next to a deep blue-green, then a stroke of gray-green to indicate a new plane, and that plane becoming blue-white where it catches the light from the window; the series of blue-whites then moving up the stalk, stopping for a series of deep reds and russet tones, to be crowned finally with a conglomeration of blue-white pinks that refer less to the light from the window than to the climax of the series of modulations. Our Monet detail may be considered an example of this latter kind of painting.

It is the scale by which the color in your painting moves, the precise nature of that articulation, that constitutes your personal expression.

The Henri Matisse painting *Interior with Etruscan Vase* is an example of a work having very large steps or contrasts of hue and pattern. Objects range from small discs of fruit to square splashes of pots to a large square of vertical mirror to a large square of horizontal table to long arches of tabletop to abrupt curves of leaves. The red curtain at the left has a scale and curves that remind us of both the vase and the seated woman.

A great range of color itself is also displayed: the close, near-blacks of the tabletop, background, and plant leaves; the abrupt color of the vase and the curtain; sharp stripes; and blurred mirror. There is both crowding and spaciousness, details and generalizations. All of this looks casual and accidental, but you will not find many modern paintings with a greater range of painterly situations. The ability to combine both a small scale and a large scale of situations on a single canvas is a special characteristic of Matisse.

Any work of art that has a wide range of sensations or "events," will have need of transitions, bridges, ways to get from one situation to another. One device of Matisse is especially interesting in this regard. When we look at the vase, we see it is a large shape of one color decorated with certain marks or designs. That inscribing with black lines, though it seems very casual and appears only to have the purpose of "activating" the surface, is really a means of combining a large form with tiny forms. The particular shape and arrangement of those marks also link the vase's designs with the thin colored lines of the woman's robe.

Notice also the handles or ears of the vase. These small black holes reappear in the box on which the vase stands and in the rungs of the table. It is no accident that these "negative spaces" are similar to the small round objects, or "positive spaces"—the fruit scattered along the table. Those bright colors in turn are linked to the larger spots of bright colors in the painting. Further inscribing with fine lines on the surface of the table and a kind of linear tracery within the foliage provide additional transitions between small and large elements in the composition. It would be wrong to call these linear motifs simple decoration; their function is entirely organic and structural.

Matthiasdottir's *Still Life* also presents us with large color changes: her steps are large and brusque, as if the artist were covering her terrain in a few huge strides. Within the overall matrix of dark green, we go abruptly from red to white to light blue to dull yellow; there are few shifts or preparatory steps between one color and another, yet there is an unfaltering firmness in the play of each color against the next.

Cham Hendon, on the other hand, seems to have no consistency: he seems to lurch. Within a general area of bright or quiet colors, many tiny steps may be evident, but then abruptly—as with the black chair among the reds, or the screaming green after a long wall of mild and close greens—we are confronted with a sudden change in the rules, a shift in the scale of color increments. This is one source of the humor or disquiet that pervades the work.

In Jensen's *Equality III Seek Their Equality*, the scale is absolutely regular. Jensen's attitude seems to be that of a scribe, patiently copying down the hieroglyphs of his tradition. Only the unfailingly full emotion delivered with each stroke, the overall liveliness and coherence of his color adjustments, distinguishes him as a true artist and not a calligrapher. In this particular instance, the equality and the individuality of each chromosome square or runic number is part of his message.

Jensen is a conceptual artist whose ideas are not really literary or mathematical; his paintings are not sketches intended to be converted into some future object or act. Whatever conversion he hoped to achieve would still lie in the realm of the intellect and of feeling, and would always depend on the quality of paint and the steadiness of scale.

Exercises

1. Set out six 1″ squares in a row; color the first with a light, bright lemon yellow and the last plain black. In four steps color the remaining squares with increasingly darker yellows to produce an even transition.

2. Do the same in eight squares.

3. Do the same in sixteen squares. You may alternate the hues between yellow and blue if you like to complicate things, but the steps of increasing darkness must be kept even. Don't expect to be satisfied on your first attempt.

P.S. Certainly a dark, blackish yellow seems a contradiction; but try to maintain the identity of the darkening yellow without veering over to green or brown or gray.

5
TONALITY

Though you want a variety of effects and qualities, you also want to sustain a continuity of color sensations that will enable the viewer to perceive the total canvas as a single entity.

Whether representational or abstract, nearly all paintings consist of a variety of shapes and colors. Still, however varied its configurations and combinations, the successful canvas will have a sense of continuity or singleness of tone by which the feeling of unity is achieved.

The painting you are building may consist of many contrasting color sensations—bright and dull, warm and cool, sweet and acid, and so on—but it is important that a certain homogeneity be maintained: despite the variety of effects or qualities, you want to sustain a certain continuity of sensation that will enable the viewer to perceive the total canvas as bearing a single attitude. The successful painting, even if it depicts a whole jumble of different objects, will still convey the sense that it is after all a single presence.

In the same way, a motion picture may present us with a great variety of actions and situations; yet something about the acting, the pacing, the photography, gives the film a distinctive style that holds it all together.

An example of singleness of tone is offered by Philip Guston's painting *Untitled, 1980.* Of the paintings in our collection, it is one of the most evenly colored: dominated by a blackish tone, its hues seem to range from dark blue-purple to dusky brown-purple, achieving only in the wedge of the sun a color that is moderately light and clear. The simply configured forms also invite a singleness of perception and reinforce the sense of monochrome which dominates the work. Later on I will show that this coherence was not, however, so easily won.

Guston's imagery is of course pure fantasy, and so it might be said that his subdued tonal range is pure invention. More traditional uses of close tonality are illustrated by the Monet, in which groups of figures are painted in close tones to convey the sense of a shaded path and care is taken that no single form or brush stroke destroys the sense of shade which is constructed to contrast with the areas of sunlight. The complexity, variety, and spontaneity of the forms within this shade make this passage in the Monet especially marvelous. Without destroying the singleness of tone, Monet gives each figure an individual role in the pageant that leads through the shade and toward the distant light, and each figure seems to exist within its own degree of shadow, half-light, or dappled sunlight.

The unity of Frank Stella's *Tahkt* is also achieved by sustained control, though his system seems relatively mechanical—consisting as it does of such devices as maintaining even widths in all the bands, separating each with a narrow border of white, and having a composition that is essentially a pattern of repetition. But the work has undeniable vitality, generated by Stella's lively, carefully controlled selection of colors. All are bright but most are only moderately intense, with colors of full power reserved for places where they serve to generate a disequilibrium within the general regularity.

Tonality or coherence can be achieved in paintings displaying a great variety of colors and forms. A work may fairly bristle with sharp contrasts and yet present itself as a single whole in which no one color or element separates itself from the others.

My own painting *Malcolm*, reproduced on the cover, deliberately consists of a wide range of distinct hues. Indeed, some of the coherence must stem from the fact that, different as the hues are, the colors are all equally bright; sharpness of contrast becomes a common denominator. Nevertheless, I had to keep the sharp array of colors subordinate to the encompassing blue of the head because the blue is called upon to provide a strong overall contrast of hue. By reason of the vigor of its own contour and its placement against the contrasting hue of yellow ochre, the blue must contain the explosion of reds, yellows, whites, and greens. The bright green area on the left, containing the woodpecker, further emphasizes the unity of the head and its background by presenting an opposition entity against which its own cohesion is affirmed.

Compared to *Malcolm*, Dufy's *Open Window*—with its many modulated blues and its subordinate patches of red—seems almost monochromatic. The nature and function of these modulations is complex, but even a quick glance tells us of the multiplicity of objects and spaces brought together by the singleness of hue. Everywhere, the artist has adjusted his blues to maintain a balance between sameness and difference. In *Open Window*, the general tone is one of quiet; in *Malcolm*, the tone is much more clamorous; but in both, the level of contrast is maintained throughout.

The tonality of de Kooning's *Asheville* is harder to define in the terms used for the other paintings. There is certainly no singleness of hue or even of contrast, since the painting exhibits a wide variety of colors; still, all are subordinated to the matrix of white. In addition, all the brushwork (so strongly evident), whether white, color, or black, is subordinated to the insistent rhythms and high energy that pervades the work.

In the end, the canvas must be described as a map of relentless energy expended in every direction. The evidence of that sustained energy binds the work together, fulfilling in *Asheville* the same function that in the work of other artists is fulfilled by the harmony of forms or the structure of color relationships.

Exercises

1. Construct on different sheets of paper three areas, 11″ × 14″ each, each in turn made up of twelve equal squares. In the first set of twelve squares, fill each square with hues of your choice, all fairly intense. Do the same for the second area, using colors having less impact. Do the same for the third, this time with even milder colors. Each area of squares, when seen from a little distance, should look uniform, with no single color popping out.

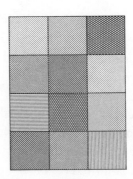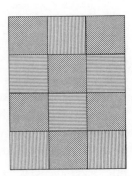

2a. Make three sets of five adjacent squares, 3″ × 3″ each. In the first set lay out the following colors in each square: orange, blue, red, green, violet. These colors will contrast strongly. In the next set of five, use the same *hues* but modify each so that the contrasts are less strong. Reduce the contrast further in the third set. Go on to a fourth row if you like, reducing the contrast even more.

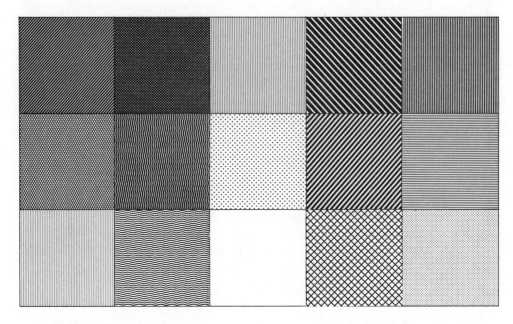

2b. Repeat the same exercise, but in the initial set use one square of black, one of white, and—if you dare—one of gray to replace three of the spectrum colors.

3a. In the center of a sheet of paper, paint a red square, 1½″ × 1½″. On another sheet of paper, paint a considerably darker red square; and on a third sheet, a red square substantially lighter than the first.

3b. Now, adjacent to each corner of the first square, paint a square of different hue but equal intensity. Do the same for each of the other reds.

6

ARTICULATION

To articulate is to present all aspects of a situation clearly, legibly, and coherently, with all parts in lucid relation to each other. The surface of your painting can present such clarity of sensation.

A person who is articulate can explain clearly all aspects of a particular situation, so that it lies before us intelligibly, with all its parts in clear relation to each other. The surface of a painting, too, can convey this clarity of sensation. I am not speaking of composition in the ordinary sense, but of the surface as an abstract presence.

The idea of articulation may be best explained by a close examination of the painting *Untitled, 1980* by Philip Guston. The main elements are easy to describe: on a slanting plane of earth occupying the lower third of the painting sits an enormous sphere, partially covering the disc of the sun, which appears to the left as a pale, peach-colored wedge upon a lavender and purplish sky.

The sun is pale, but compared to the dark somber tones of the rest of the painting, it can be described as almost bright. The painting is indeed characterized by this severe contrast, and our examination should focus on the elements by which this opposition is mediated. Although the contrast is sharp where the spherical rock abuts the sun, elsewhere the contrasts are less insistent, and it is this integration between bright and somber that gives the painting its sense of inevitability.

The slab of earth, which is even darker (and warmer) than the rock, lightens somewhat and becomes substantially warmer at the lower left where it abuts the wedge of the sun. Surrounding the curving edge of the sun is a lavender tone whose middle value, as well as its hue, affords substantial but quiet contrast. Above, still at the left, the sky darkens by means of an increasing incidence of purplish blue, which as a solid color moves rightward above the rock and joins the somber hues dominating not only the right side of the painting but the picture generally. In this way the abruptness of contrast between sun and rock is cushioned by precise modifications of surrounding colors.

In terms of hue and of warm and cool juxtapositions, Guston's painting may be described simply as warm (reddish) earth and sun, and cool (bluish) rock and sky. In this context, the lavender may be described as intermediate in the hue scale (lavender is light violet, and violet is a combination of red and blue); it may also be called intermediate in the warm-cool scale and in the value scale.

The power of this small (23" × 29") painting, therefore, derives as much from the simple firmness of its tonal and color relationships as from its simple yet cosmic image: it displays masterful articulation in its mediation between two entities.

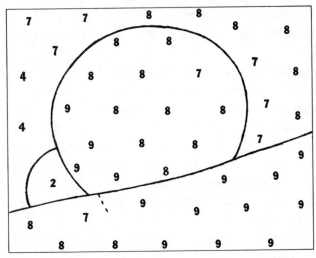

6-1. Juxtapositions of value can be diagrammed as a series of numbers, in which 1 is assigned to white and 10 to black.

An important aspect of articulation is the quality of "breathing" that a successful painting imparts. This quality echoes our sense of rhythmic alternation—the in and out of breath, the rise and fall of waves, the system of pulsation by which so much of the energy we experience manifests itself. (On another level this may be spoken of as yin and yang, the principle of inevitably linked complements.)

Looking more closely at the Guston painting, we notice emanating from the sun not only black lines but whitish cloudlets, which carry some of the lightness of the sun into the middle tone of the sky and at the same time set up a rhythm within the lavender in preparation for the darker cloudlets above. The huge spherical rock is surfaced with similar dabs of energy, short ink lines of black that roughen the surface and articulate the variations of form, and also provide continuity among the clouds, the rock, and the drawing of the shoe. The drawn foot, whatever its symbolic meaning, is a shape clearly reminiscent of the sun and indeed of the play of irregular circles against straight lines which constitutes the formal leitmotif of the work. Through all these elements surges a recurrent pulsation whose energy is an important source of the painting's unity and liveliness.

One acknowledged masterpiece of quiet yet powerful articulation is *Man with Crossed Arms* by Paul Cézanne. Our color reproduction shows only the head, so we cannot here speak of the composition; but we can examine in detail the complete fugue of the brush strokes that constitute the face.

In general, the colors of the face descend from a very high—that is, a very light—yellowish red, to a deeper but not very intense red at the cheeks, to tones becoming violet as the red becomes increasingly charged with blue. On the whole, the colors are moderate, never bright, and the changes or modulations are gradual and never severe.

As we examine the modulations of tone that characterize the face, we notice especially the oscillation between warm and cool. Sometimes red is fairly dramatically juxtaposed against blue, but more often the pulsation consists of small but repeated shifts: one brush stroke is a trifle warmer, the next a trifle cooler, so that

Paul Cézanne *Man with Crossed Arms*. Oil on canvas, 1899
(36¼ × 28⅝ inches). The Solomon R. Guggenheim Museum, New York.
Photo: David Heald

a sense of vibrancy is sustained throughout. Each pulse of energy shares company with one of rest.

We may classify the shifts of color as alterations of hue, alterations of brightness, or alterations of value (light and dark). The shifts of color become greater where the change of plane or form is greater.

It is particularly instructive to see how a relatively abrupt shift of color, crowning a sustained series of small changes, conveys the sense of a sharp break in form in the fold of the cheek just above the nostril on our left: a dab of bright orange-red put next to a dusky bluish red. A larger protuberance of form is the cheekbone on our right, where the sustained bright red lifts the form from the light cool tones of the distant contour and from the near hollow of the cheek (indicated by more violet tones).

Conversely, an extended sweep of form is conveyed by the long series of barely shifting colors of which the forehead above the eye to our right is composed: the pale whitish strokes along the far periphery become increasingly warm until the dabs become a rich peach color where they meet the stronger colors of the peak of the eyebrow. A series of small shifts of warm color conveys the hardness across the front of the forehead, until the advent of increasingly blue tones marks the change to the side of the head.

The jumble of violet tones and warm reds composing the chin coalesces, if you squint, into a very strong form with a definite sheen among the half-lights, and even creates a slim highlight before your eye moves into the strongly articulated but always darker tones of the neck.

The two eyes differ intriguingly from each other and by their difference suggest an unexpected distance across the face, as if we had traveled from one situation to another. Moreover, the sinking of the eye on our right, by its dark color, allows the eye on our left with its stronger contrast to become a second, stronger beat and makes the man's gaze more abrupt and focused. This push of the eyeball is reflected in the forms just below the eye, which look like the wake of a fast-traveling boat.

This expressiveness is a quality not generally associated with Cézanne, but it is one of the results of the artist's assiduous observation and his determination to match every movement of his own eye, by which he perceived the particulars of form, with a corresponding shift of color on his canvas. We may know the two eyes of the man in the painting are alike, but in our perception each is varied and individual.

The articulation of color in my portrait sketch of Leo Steinberg is of a very different scale from Cézanne's portrait.* Whereas Cézanne's strokes hover around a central warm tonality, the strokes of paint in my sketch jump from dark red to light blue and from bright yellow to black and pale green. Yet this wide disparity of hue resides within an overall matrix of light blue that constitutes both the foundation of the face and the background itself.

To speak of the face in *Portrait of Leo Steinberg* as a landscape, bluffs and hollows are indicated without the intermediate steps that make up the whole configuration always being specified. The nose appears as a yellow crest emerging out of the mild blue and set against the sharper purple-red of the eye socket. The warmer and more diffused patch of yellow climaxes the forehead, but it appears out of the pale blue matrix without any specific articulation of its structure beyond the reddish contour and the surround of hair.

My intention of course, is considerably different from Cézanne's. His was to maintain the integrity of the three-dimensional solid despite his use of fragmented brush strokes; mine is to suggest solidity but essentially to dissolve the form into nearer equality with the overall matrix. Thus the flow of the brush depicting the hair and the back of the head retains a certain calligraphic character that flattens the form, just as the blue facade of the face—with its detail of lips and nostrils—which would normally be perceived as receding toward the left, appears to flatten so that it is parallel with the picture plane: the imaginary window-pane of the canvas itself. This is comparable to the practice of certain

*Both color reproductions are details of the originals; in mine, a continuation of light blue on either side has been chopped off; in the Cézanne, the whole dark mass of the body and the fairly strong blue of the background—both important counters to the warm light tones of the face—have been eliminated.

classical Chinese landscape painters who arranged receding "layers" of mountains (set in an overall mist) in such a way as to allow each mountain, whether near or far, to be perceived with equal impact while retaining the overall scheme of deep vistas.

Articulation in Stella's piece and in Jensen's is programmed, consisting of very regular changes or—more precisely put—of changes that fall into a clearly apparent format. Stella permits himself to assign various colors to the circular bands, but the format and proportions of the bands do not change. When we look at the Stella, it seems simple and we think we perceive all its workings at once: nothing could be clearer. Yet the colors are carefully adjusted, and we find them full of subtle pulls and balances. They manage to sustain a sense of breathing in and out.

Similarly, Jensen's checkerboard format seems nonnegotiable: the artist himself always claimed the format and even the colors were a given. Yet the remarkable coherence of the piece speaks of a visual sensibility, as well as a surprising liveliness, and these are not qualities we expect in a scientific chart; there is no mistaking that this is an organic work of art. The colors give us a sense of continuous, alternating push and release across the entire surface.

In contrast, Frankenthaler's method in *Aries* seems to permit almost no premeditation about format, and her shapes of color seem given over to chance—the artist allowing that procedure of pouring and staining to determine the composition of her work. The nature and degree of articulation seem largely determined by chance, though certainly she mixes her colors carefully before pouring them and can determine to a degree the number and extension of the stains. Each impulse of color, no matter how full, is allowed eventually to decay, like a single note struck on a piano, before another note of color is sounded.

As the sense of implacability is a hallmark of Jensen's work, so the quality of minimum intercession is the hallmark of Frankenthaler's. The brightness of her stains never interferes with our awareness of the raw canvas; the whole becomes a metaphor for a provisional, transient universe.

Finally, we need to notice the remarkable clarity of the de Kooning, which though entirely spontaneous and seemingly haphazard in approach and composition, allows us to see every nuance of color and every lash of black as if under the bright lights of an operating table. His use of white is quite different from Stella's. Whereas Stella's intervals of white provide a neutral base from which each separate color may exist in relative isolation, de Kooning's white is everywhere engaged. The white is always coming out of or going into a condition of color; it is always a partner with the streaks and splashes of black, sometimes playing an active role, sometimes a passive one. Remembering Harold Rosenberg's observation of "meaning grasped and lost" in this kind of painting, we can see the white as a primal factor in building and dissolving these elusive forms. The sharpness of black against white, however, and the clarity of color against white both increase the illusion of comprehensibility, thus heightening the sense—frustrating, perhaps—that these forms are indeed within our grasp.

Exercises

1. Paint three bands of blue adjacent to each other: a medium blue, a somewhat lighter blue, and then a pale blue.

Now paint a second group of blues: a medium blue, a lighter blue that contains a touch of violet, and then a blue that is still lighter and this time contains a touch of green or aqua. This succession of blues will not blend so easily as the first; the eye will perceive differences in clarity or articulation, even at a substantial distance.

2. Do the same exercise for the hues red and green.

3. Make a pattern consisting of six small discs of one color against a background of another. The colors should contrast in hue but not in value. Now, to sharpen the differentiation between discs and background, do the following, without resorting to contrast of value: paint a dot in each disc; paint rims around the discs; paint lines on the background in a diamond pattern. After each procedure notice how much more sharply the basic pattern is articulated.

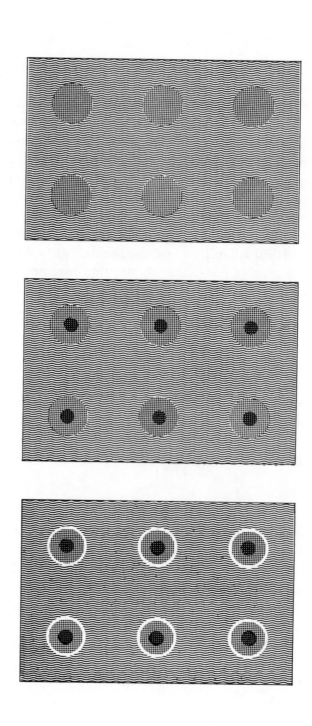

7

A SURVEY OF STRUCTURES

It is important to think systematically about the organization and use of
color in your paintings.

Our discussions, which thus far have mainly been concerned with the structural
use of color in painting, may now be summarized and reviewed. Perhaps the best
method for doing this is a procedure borrowed from the practice of painting
itself. Most of us, at one time or another in the process of developing a painting,
have recourse to looking at the work with half-closed eyes—for by squinting we
blur details and see the work more simply, as if from a distance.

So, let us turn to the color reproductions of our paintings and, as if we were
seeing them from a great distance, imagine we are looking at all of them at once. If
we compare them, reduced and simplified in this way, we will see more emphati-
cally than ever the wide range of color structures we have been studying.

Then let us try to describe in the briefest way possible the color strategy that
characterizes each work. It is clear that even a minimum description must
designate the organization that holds the work together—must go beyond the
simple naming of dominant colors. "Variations of blue" or "dark green plus four
other colors" may be true descriptions, but they do not designate any principle of
cohesion.

Here is my list of formulations—a list produced by squeezing my eyes.
After you have read mine, I invite you to choose another group of paintings and
produce your own list of thumbnail descriptions.

Color Structures—Hues

1. Mondrian: Primary colors, full strength, arranged adjacently against white and gray.

2. Picasso: The primary triad: the red full-strength, the yellow lighter, the blue quite pale. This combined with black and white and arranged in a system of oppositions.

3. de Kooning: Light to bright colors imbedded in a matrix of white slashed with black.

4. Matthiasdottir: Fairly bright chunks of color, isolated and set against a matrix of dark green.

5. Matisse: Splashes of color subtly interconnected in a ground of black and green.

6. Dufy: Monochrome of closely shaded blues, relieved with red and touches of green and whitish blue.

7. Guston: A close assortment of dark dull blues and dark dull reds, relieved by a wedge of pink.

8. Kriesberg (*Malcolm*): Assortment of bright colors nested in deep blue, nested in dull yellow.

9. Frankenthaler: Firm primary colors, in a context of diluted primaries.

10. Stella: Sixteen bands of mostly warm colors.

11. Monet: Mostly violet and green, modulated to create depth.

And compressing our eyes even further, we might label our paintings in the following way:

COLOR STRUCTURES – ENERGY

Artist	Configuration	Energy System
1. Mondrian	Paths and Stations	Linear
2. Picasso	Opposition and Resolution	Juxtapositional
3. de Kooning	Fragmentation	Cyclonic
4. Matthiasdottir	Isolated Jewels	Balanced
5. Matisse	Mutually Opposing Systems	Interweaving
6. Dufy	Variations of Single Color	Faceted
7. Guston	Interlocked Gears	Rotary
8. Kriesberg	Nested and Mirrored	Confined Explosion
9. Frankenthaler	Centralization Collapsed	Spreading
10. Stella	Even Adjacencies	Repetition
11. Monet	Light and Shade	Traversing

Trying to tag a complex work of art with a single word or phrase can easily become just a game, of course; but if on the one hand you do not approach the idea too flippantly, and if on the other you refrain from taking a doctrinaire attitude toward such designations, you will find the game a very good way to exercise your mind's eye. Any systematic way of looking is useful. I recommend that you select, as an exercise, a different set of ten works and develop your own system of tags for them. The formulations may need to be reduced in stages.

Perhaps these labeling exercises have suggested to you certain generalizations or principles of color organization. You need not push each work into a particular category, and certainly the works should not be continued in those places permanently. The exercises simply give you some analytic handles. You may see that some paintings are more monochromatic than others, that some oppose spots of color against a matrix, and that others make no such play. Some resist answers and ask questions instead: for example, the Frankenthaler, it could be said, does not at first seem to oppose colors against matrix; yet the original painting—if not the reproduction—insistently makes us aware of the bare canvas; is that a matrix?

One observation we can make with some certainty is that, whereas older works achieved their unity by a system of connections or by the subordination of part to whole, modern works tend to consist of autonomous elements that are juxtaposed rather than harmonized.

Our oldest painting, the Monet, was done in 1887. Modernity is of course relative, and Monet, as an Impressionist, worked in a manner that most people would call modern. Every square inch of the little canvas is filled with a marvelous array of colors, yet the range of hues and tones is subordinated to the general condition of the colors' presence in light or shade. And in terms of its structure or organization, Monet's painting is quite traditional, for its composition depends upon a strict subordination of part to whole.

In an earlier chapter I discussed the play between horizontal and vertical elements in the Monet as the basic scheme of the painting. The components—paths, people, foliage, building, even foreground and distance—all perform their assigned roles in this scheme, like actors in a stage drama.

The colors build from quiet to climax, and all the details of figure and dress are subject to the overall movement from deep shadow to flecked half-light to bright sunshine.

Before proceeding to the question of contemporary modes of construction, it will be useful to examine our other nineteenth century painting, the portrait by Cézanne. The triumph of Western painting in the fourteenth century included the development of depiction with light and shade, making possible the portrayal of convincingly solid forms that received light and threw shadows. In general this created a system in which the components that received light were more important than those that fell in shadow. Impressionist painting changed this by investing shadowy portions with as much color and articulation as sunlit portions possessed.

Cézanne's portrait throws much of the man's face into a kind of half-shadow, but there is certainly no longer a system of subordination of one section to another. All strokes of paint play an equal role in the building of that fugue of color. In my *Portrait of Leo Steinberg*, similarly, the patch of yellow which is the nose may refer to light and the area of purple which is the eye socket may refer to shadow, but they are both equal patches of color.

In terms of composition, the Matisse, a twentieth century painting, is much more problematic than the Monet, even though in its own way it also depends on a system of tight relationships. The elements in the Matisse, however, tend to have a status of equality rather than subordination. In Picasso's composition *The Studio*, no system of subordinations or even of connections exists: we have instead a play of oppositions.

In the Frankenthaler, too, we cannot speak of subordination or connection. Juxtaposition seems a more apt description of its composition. In her painting, each area is a flooded color that sustains and extends itself until it meets another abstract presence of color, each with its own degree of resilience, affirmation, or tentativeness.

In the chapter on tension, I described how Elizabeth Murray's painted construction *Back on Earth* is built on a system of opposing entities.

Stella's painting *Tahkt-I-Sulayman Variation 1* is a work that very frankly consists of oppositions or (more precisely) adjacencies: adjacent bands arranged in a format of two squares set side by side. The patterns of the two halves are identical, except that one is rotated a quarter turn and the bands have been assigned different colors in the two squares. Considering the mechanical arrangement of this composition, the resulting combination is quite lively and varied.

The principle of color relationship may here be described as variation, a principle quite common in musical composition. Although the word "variation" in Stella's title refers to the several variably colored versions of this work with the identical pattern, the word also refers to the system of coherence in the work itself, which is, in general terms, the simple repetition of equals.

These "protractor" paintings by Stella, seen in the original, are quite impressive. They are very large and, painted in fluorescent acrylic, the color possesses a very distinct quality of splendor. The large scale and the fluorescent sheen are lost in reproduction, but the white lines between the colors are not, and they account to a large extent for the brilliance and clarity in the work. Lest I be thought to give too much credit to simple mechanical devices, let me emphasize that the color arrangements—or to be more precise, the color allotments—are in themselves ingenious, invigorating, and resonant.

The appeal of this work stems not only from its sensate handsomeness, but from its coolness as well—the live-and-let-live of its composition or format. It says in effect, "Here I am; make of me whatever you will." The viewer, confronting this, feels a certain freedom and exhilaration. By contrast, the marvelous articulation of the Monet imposes upon us the necessity to follow the brush strokes carefully. Not only must our eye read the strokes as figure, foliage, and path, but it must also notice how every brushstroke of color impinges upon several others. Consciously or not, our eye is negotiating countless relationships, and if we are to look closely, our eye must allow itself to be managed quite strictly. Not so, the Stella; here, while the eye does take in the total ensemble, each color can be seen without the complexities of subtle abutments. Indeed, we feel we can choose which color to savor, when and how we please.

The role of color could not differ more completely than it does in the hands of these two artists.

Exercises

With regard to your own work, I do not suggest that you base your next painting on a predesignated scheme or system—one of the tags we listed earlier in this chapter. You must of course approach your own work in your own way, and no one can tell you precisely how to combine your intuition, your feelings, and your intelligence.* No system or scheme can ensure the making of a unified and lively painting, but I do recommend that you ask yourself, during the course of your work, certain questions that may help you to look at your canvas in a more cohesive way. Sometimes, drawing diagrams of these structures will be helpful. Do not be concerned if you cannot determine conclusively a category into which your painting falls. These designations are only devices for thinking more analytically.

In the actual work of art, no system is ever absolute or exclusive. After all, the act of painting does not consist of simply executing a preconceived plan. Every work in progress has the potential to suggest to the artist new, sometimes divergent or even contradictory ideas for the finished work.

1. Is the work chiefly monochromatic or is it quite varied in color?

2. In "temperature," are the colors predominantly warm or cool?

3. In value, are the colors close to each other or varied?

4. Does the work move from one color to another smoothly or abruptly?

5. Are the color contrasts mostly toward the top, toward the bottom, or along one side, or are they evenly distributed?

6. Are the colors contrasting, generally opposed, or parallel to each other? That is, are the colors woven together so they mingle, or do they stand apart in different areas of the canvas?

7. If there is a dominant color area or object, how are the other objects or areas related to it: in hue? in value? in texture? Do the subsidiary colors build toward the dominant color or oppose it?

---

*Not only is it impossible for one person to prescribe for another just how to proceed in making a painting, individual artists themselves give conflicting reports of their own approach. For example, Miró, in 1941 said, "Let the works be conceived in a frenzy, but carried out with clinical coolness." In 1959, however, he described a different mode of execution, saying, "I work in a state of passion and compulsion."

8

TEMPERAMENT

Temperament involves the intimations of paint. The surface of the painting shows what is inside us and reflects an individual persona.

Beneath the obvious differences in subject matter and style among the artists we are studying here lies the more fundamental difference of temperament. Each artist has a very distinctive intention or reason for painting. This intention need not be "before" the artist as work begins, and indeed it need not be consciously recognized even after the painting is finished. The artistic expression of fundamental temperament is less often the result of a deliberate decision than of an unconscious insistence that the work reflect the artist's individuality or disposition.

The marvelous thing is that these qualities of temperament show up in paint. Even more remarkably, there is usually a consensus among the viewing public about the particular temperament or personality being expressed. The individual temperament manifests itself in the quality of paint application, and sometimes the way the paint has come onto the canvas is more telling than the particular structure of the composition.

In art, paint is never just paint: the de Kooning is not just a collection of paint smears, the Stella is not just a bunch of stripes, and, for that matter, the Monet is not just some people in a park. On a canvas, any given area possesses a certain specific vibrancy, whether it serves to produce a sense of calm or ruggedness or lightness. All the elements on the whole canvas have a certain degree of substantiality, whether soft or hard; they may feel as obdurate as steel or rock, or they may seem as evanescent as clouds. They may seem emblematic or hieroglyphic and thus outside the realm of materiality. These qualities become apparent not only through pictorial composition but also through the manner in which the paint is handled by the artist.

When we look at the Dufy, we know we are looking at table, rug, sky, and sea; and yet at the same time we know we are looking at brush marks of blue paint or of green. Furthermore, we are aware, by those marks of paint, of the particular personality of the artist. Our mind's negotiating of those three sorts of awareness gives us the pleasure of looking at the picture.

The particular quality of lightness, of deftness—the dash and felicity of line, as well as the resonance of color that characterizes this particular piece—characterizes also, we know, the whole life's work of this artist.* Not only do all of his works possess these qualities, but every part of each work displays them. Sky and sea are not less dense than sofa or wardrobe. Look at any work by Raoul Dufy, whether it shows a vase of flowers, horses at the paddock, or a curve of the French Riviera, and you will feel essentially the same deftness, the same buoyancy, the same resonance of color.

The oeuvre of Henri Matisse is more varied, ranging from solidly painted figures to paper cutouts. In his most characteristic style, however, exemplified in our selection, we are struck by a casualness that masks an amazing complexity, a deftness that somehow generates a sense of firmness, and a degree of gravity perhaps absent from Dufy.

In the Matisse, all the objects—table, plants, figure, bases, floor, curtain—have the same degree of lightness, firmness, and eventual gravity.

In the Matthiasdottir, the whole painting feels solid and hard, as if we were looking at a terrain full of boulders. In contrast, the whole Frankenthaler seems provisional, without weight or permanence; despite its bright colors, everything

*The fine lines that show around the balcony are existing cracks in the paint. However sublime a painting may be, it is never quite immortal.

in the painting seems distant and calm. In the de Kooning, the actual forms seem no more certain, but the physical sense is totally different.

This quality of paint and temperament has to do with the whole canvas perceived as a single entity, and it stems not from the subject matter but from the innate disposition of the artist.

Further distinctions can be made. The Frankenthaler breathes a certain exhilaration, but it is a contained exhilaration—not at all like the lyric frenzy of a Jackson Pollock. Frankenthaler's clouds of color though somewhat similar, are lighter and less insistent than the areas of resonant color scumbled up by Mark Rothko, which envelope us completely as we stand in front of his paintings. Alfred Jensen's painting has a format as fixed and geometric as Frank Stella's, but the thick, squirming worms that are his marks are as different as they can possibly be from Stella's processed look and majestic but cool elegance. The Elizabeth Murray is tough, jaunty, and palpable; yet despite the physicality of its structure and the lively experience it offers, its visual actuality is much lighter than the de Kooning which obliges us to use our eye like a plow and indeed, with its smoldering high energy, invokes our pulse as much as our eye.

The actual process of paint application does not in itself ensure a particular emotional reading. That the Frankenthaler consists of paint poured freely onto raw canvas is one source of our sense of exhilaration. A very different feeling, evoked by a similar process, can be illuminated by looking closely at the interior painted by Cham Hendon: many of the objects, including the complex surface of the tabletop, were produced by pouring one wet color into another. These color areas, as carefully confined as those in a child's coloring book, have a definite palpability, as though they were just so many diligent craft objects; and our eye is held to the ground, with no chance of soaring. Hendon practices a variation of the Pop aesthetic: no distinction is conceded between the object and its depiction. In the painting, the tabletop is an area of poured paint, just as in real life the table was actually made of poured epoxy to imitate marble.

Elizabeth Murray's construction contains another variation of pouring or near pouring. The light green pattern that appears on top of the dark green may have been applied with a brush, but its contour, particularly the squiggle at the

60   Working With Color

bottom, is clearly derived from the pouring process. In this work, the manner of paint application is less important than the contours, which echo the curves and half-moons of the cutouts. In turn, the swing and energy of the cutout contours derive from the free experience of pouring.

Such close looking and careful articulation of response must be part of our awareness as viewers and as artists. Just as tone of voice may tell us more about a speaker's meaning than actual words do, the feeling of paint can sometimes reveal more to us than subject matter or composition.

The paintings of Jensen and Cézanne are as different as we can possibly imagine. Their format is different, and their artistic philosophy was different. Cézanne said he worked from nature, and in fact a model posed for him; Jensen said he worked from a system and in fact he referred to a modern chromosome chart or an ancient runic text. Yet both artists worked in a sustained and even mosaic of paint dabs with a patience and a dedication to an ideal that speaks of a more common temperament than their very different formats and ideologies would at first suggest. The particular temper of their paint application should perhaps command our attention as much as the resulting pictorial coherence or composition.

A final word on this subject to the working artist. Although I believe that the individual temper of the artist is crucial to the particular character of our work, I do not want to suggest that you or I as artists should stand in front of our easel and contemplate our personality or temperament. Thinking about our personality may be useful for some enterprises, but I don't advocate it as part of the process of painting. It is not simply that one's real temper is always unconscious, but that the personality perceived in a work (and to which I have been alluding) is the persona of the artist as revealed in his or her work. That is no assurance that in real life the artist has that particular character.

I am willing to say that, whereas Matisse sees an interior as a glowing flight of themes and variations, Cham Hendon sees an interior as a series of pratfalls, each marked by an object of ignominious color. I am not able to assure you, however, that sharing a luncheon table with us, Matisse would have proved an estatic companion or that Hendon would provide rollicking entertainment.

Imagine that we are watching a particular mime perform: we see him pose as a lover, a soldier, a fool; but always he is a mime—we know it and he knows it. Whatever he expresses as a lover, he must project silently, without props, solely by the stance and movements of his body. Painting is not a performing art, and yet the painter must play that same double role—as one who feels passions but is detached enough to express them with perfected craft. The artist's expression must be projected in terms of a particular format of color, shape, and interval, and must reveal itself in the paint that covers a flat, inert surface.

That compound of passion and objectivity—the unconscious and the conscious—must function simultaneously as we work: it is the inescapable demand of art.

Exercises

I will not ask you, in connection with this chapter, to go to your easel and paint a Frankenthaler; then, three days later, to paint a de Kooning; and three days after that, a Stella. I do, however, suggest that you look at the last few paintings you've done and ask yourself: of all the artists' works reproduced and discussed in this book, which is closest to your own work? I do not want you to compare subject matter or style, but rather the materiality of the elements on the canvas— their degree of corporality. Can you rub them between your fingers? Do you need to hustle them with both arms? Can you cut them with a knife? Does the painting convey an absence of substantiality?

1. Line up four squares and fill each with color. Now line up another four, and fill them with the same hues, this time altering the color so as to suggest that the second four are plates of steel. Now line up another four, filling them in such a way that they look like windows onto colored vapor.

Of course, different colors suggest different psychological moods or qualities. The problem is that what a particular color suggests is wholly dependent on the personal associations and temperament of the individual viewer, so no useful generalization can be made on the issue. As an exercise in extending and sharpening your response to color, though, I think it is a very good idea to attach in your mind an emotional attribute to every color you see. Some people—I am one of them—like to use personal adjectives in describing colors: "boiling" purple, for example, or "brittle" orange, or "gritty" yellow. The reason I like to use such terms is not because I believe I can thereby convey to your mind's eye precisely the color I am seeing in mine, but because in the realm of art, color always carries a feeling and always exists in a context. My purpose is not to get you to see colors as I do, but to increase your awareness of what your own eyes are seeing.

2a. Make four squares of color 2½″ × 2¼″ along the top of your sheet.

2b. Below each of the squares add four more of the same size.

2c. On the top row, fill the squares as follows: yellow, red, green, blue.

2d. Continue succeeding squares with the same hues, but modified to fulfill your notion of the idea of "pestilential" yellow, red, green, blue; "muscular" yellow, etc; "sober" yellow, etc; "brash" yellow, etc.

9

SIGNIFICATION

Meaning in painting is expressed in large part by the painterly surface
and by the use of color.

Since this is a handbook for the working artist, I have tried to talk only about
matters that are directly useful to the artist. I have not avoided opinions and
enthusiasms, and I have encouraged you to express your own. At the same time,
I have tried to stay away from general judgments.

Yet common sense tells us that we must at times assess the work we are
looking at for meaning and make some judgment concerning the values this or
that work expresses. Whereas hue is the first and most superficial aspect of a patch
of color, meaning is that color's final, unavoidable aspect.

So, too, for the whole canvas: we must each try to judge what issues the
artist is raising and how important they are. This is one of the reasons the Cham
Hendon work is so provocative. I will speak of that, but first let me turn to the
Dufy. Raoul Dufy is sometimes dismissed as essentially a stylish, decorative
painter whose charm is only too apparent. Yet if we look closely at his work, we
can often see surprising firmness and mystery. Our particular painting by Dufy
is actually quite subversive, for it neatly demonstrates the futility of any large
generalizations about art. In the matter of "color theory," it demolishes the
widely proclaimed principle that blue is recessive and red is a color that "comes
forward." In this little painting the color of the foreground table is as blue as the
color of the distant sea; and the distant red roofs are as red as the nearby sofa.

Moreover, the painting, with its seemingly unpremeditated subject and its

Claude Monet, *Parisians Enjoying the Parc Monceau* (detail). Oil on canvas, 1878 ($28^5/_8 \times 21^3/_8$ inches).
(The Metropolitan Museum of Art, Mr. and Mrs. Henry Ittleson, Jr., Fund, 1959.)

Paul Cézanne, *Man with Crossed Arms* (detail). Oil on canvas, 1899 (36¼ × 28⅝ inches).
(The Solomon R. Guggenheim Museum, New York. Photo: David Heald.)

Raoul Dufy, *Open Window, Nice*. Oil on canvas, 1928 (25½ × 21⁵/₁₆ inches). (Collection, Art Institute of Chicago.)

Pablo Picasso, *The Studio*. Oil on canvas, 1928 (59 × 91 inches).
(Collection, The Museum of Modern Art, New York. Gift of Walter P. Chrysler, Jr.)

Henri Matisse, *Interior with Etruscan Vase*. Oil on canvas, 1940 (29 × 39½ inches).
(The Cleveland Museum of Art, Gift of Hanna Fund.)

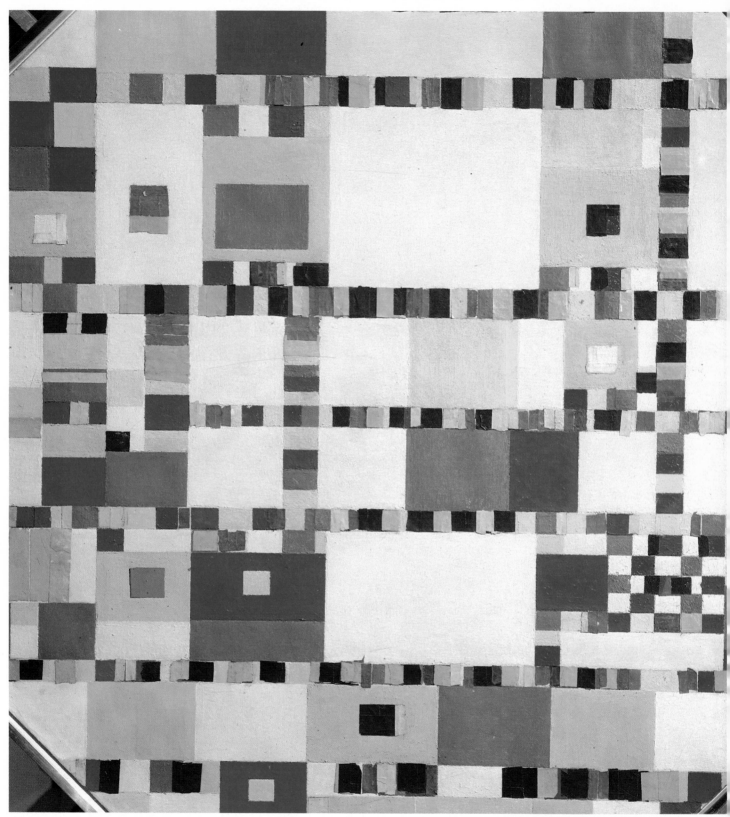

Piet Mondrian, *Victory Boogie Woogie* (detail). Oil and tape on canvas, 1944, unfinished (50 × 50 inches). (Collection, Mr. and Mrs. Burton Tremaine.)

Willem de Kooning, *Asheville*. Oil on canvas, 1949 (25⅝ × 31⅞ inches).
(The Phillips Collection, Washington, D.C.; acquired from Vincent Melzac, Virginia, 1952.)

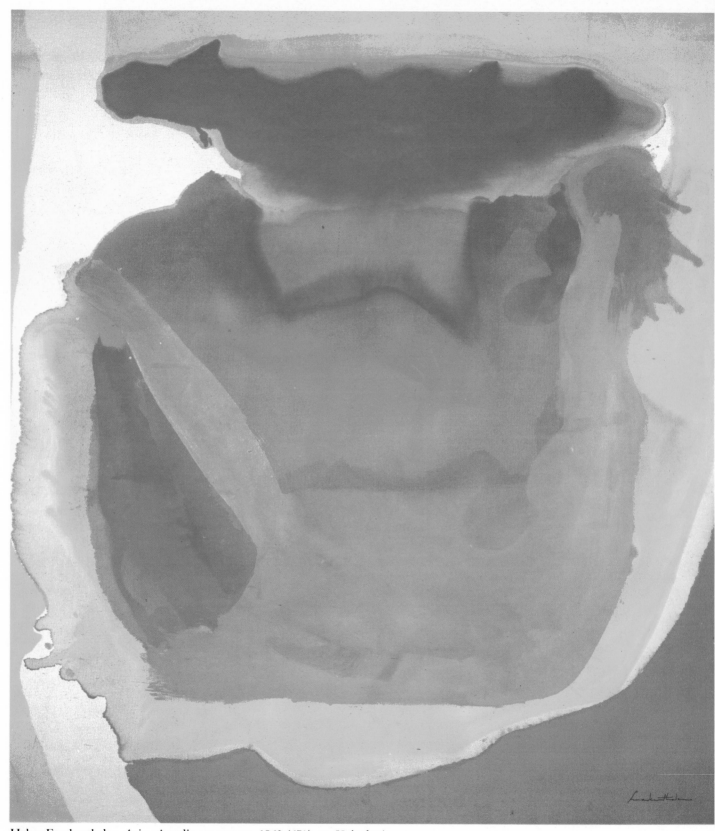

Helen Frankenthaler, *Aries*. Acrylic on canvas, 1963 (67½ × 59 inches).
(Courtesy of the artist.)

very casual painting manner, belies the idea that profound works of art must be labored tightly or must address exalted subject matter.

Open Window, Nice could be described as a philosophic work, since it takes up the theme of surfaces and of perceived reality and puts them through permutations that are as resonant to the mind as they are to the eye. Consider, as examples of perceived reality, the surface of the table, the surface of the sea, the surface of the sky, the surface of the wardrobe mirror, and, if you will, the "surface" of space, which is the open window. In what ways, we are obliged to ask, do they differ in the painting, and in what ways do they differ in reality? To answer, we must distinguish further the marks that inform the structures of the distant village and the marks that describe the pattern on a cloth or wallpaper. They are the same, and yet they are not. Then, too, if the green of the fence at the window is the same green as that of the fence in the mirror—but simply juxtaposed against different blues—what are we to think of the idea of sameness and difference altogether?

Of course, these disturbing questions of ontological ambivalence would not have been projected at all if the technical reality—the readily apparent brushwork everywhere—were not actually as equivalent as it is expressive, if the colors were not absolutely tuned to each other so that they balance on the edge between sameness and difference.

As for Cham Hendon's work, I confess I find the issues he raises very disturbing in a different arena. Comparing the Dufy interior with the Hendon, I find the first philosophic and the second satirical. Is this because subconsciously I believe a balcony view of the Mediterranean more conducive to serious reflection than a living room in Brooklyn? Is tacky furniture a less worthy subject than tasteful furnishings? What do those terms mean, anyway? Is a composition that comes to rest and equilibrium more worthy than one that seems permanently askew? Is one more true than the other? If Hendon's work offends my conservative sensibility, is that a reason to condemn it—or me? Are these, finally, appropriate questions to ask of a work of art?

I think I am unalterably persuaded that the Dufy is a more abstract work, that it addresses reality on a deeper level than the Hendon does. But is the Dufy therefore a better work of art? What does the word "better" mean: more enjoyable? more susceptible to analysis? I will stop; you may continue with questions of your own.

In the same vein, let us consider the Matthiasdottir still life. Although its subject matter is as mundane as the Hendon's, the Matthiasdottir has a very different resonance.

The artist is undeniably insistent that a cucumber is a cucumber and a pepper a pepper. But why, then, did it strike me, the first moment I saw this painting, that the cucumber was a whale? There was something about its magnitude, its mass, its sense of weight: no bright highlights to make us think of surface; only just enough light to indicate its mass . . . and the deepness of its green, and its readiness to merge, undifferentiated, with that whole matrix of green—which may indeed be a tabletop, but which curves above like the horizon at sea, echoing the hump of the whale. Is that a napkin or a towel? It is stiff and unrelenting as a sail . . .

The cheeses and pepper are very real, of course, but the squarish glass dome that separates cheese from vegetable echoes the pepper in shape and highlights and generalizes both into abstract entities. The glass dome does something further: the two cheeses and the pepper are all about the same size and are aligned with each other. The glass case differentiates the first two from the third (while echoing and augmenting the third), and it establishes an entity that equals in size that other fragile stiffness, the sail-napkin at the left.

Matthiasdottir does not hesitate to crowd her table-ocean, leaving only narrow channels free, but she provides too the slim vessel of a knife that might navigate that channel of blackish green in the center, or those other narrow, dark straits to the left and to the right.

Nothing in the Matthiasdottir's subject matter confesses to any but kitchen concerns, but everywhere in the picture intimations lurk of something more than a mere collection of objects on a table. I think the word "grandeur" here may not be inappropriate.

The majesty of the Stella is of a different order. To give it its due, we must keep in mind that the original, with its large size and fluorescent tones, is much more significantly altered by our reproduction than is the Matthiasdottir. Still, we have every right to question to what extent and in what ways the Stella resonates beyond its immediate presentation. If you prefer to compare works of more nearly the same tradition, we can look at it alongside the work of another artist of sensate qualities, Piet Mondrian.

Yet as soon as we speak of tradition, which we must, we run into certain issues that make comparisons not really so simple. Forty years separate the work of Stella from that of Mondrian, and in the twentieth century, forty years is a long time. Mondrian worked a major innovation in the tradition of Western painting; it might be said that nothing like his kind of work had existed before. Yet when compared to the Stella, several old ideas are apparent in the Mondrian. The idea of a contrapuntal composition, the hallmark of Western painting since 1400, still remains, however altered and attenuated. The idea of a canvas held in tension by painterly forces also remains.

In the Stella these qualities are gone. Has anything replaced them? Un-doubtedly;* but the problem with very new works is that we do not really perceive all that they are about—even the artist doesn't—because, indeed, we can't know their meaning or significance until we see some later developments. Therefore, we can say now that Mondrian made Stella possible, but we cannot yet make such a statement about the younger man.

We have some hints, and each of us will have to decide how important these suggestions are. Pictorial composition is gone. Indeed, during the 1960s, Stella, as a visiting artist to Yale's Graduate School of Art, spread consternation among students when he continually confronted them with the challenge "Are you still painting compositions!" (Some years later, with his large relief works, Stella himself returned to contrapuntal composition.)

In *Tahkt*, majesty stems from the artist's purely sensory presentation. Almost entirely devoid of reference and relation, this pattern of color and

*I have indicated some of these new qualities in Chapter 7.

form—simple, absolute, isolated—stirs feelings and attitudes in us that can leave us breathless and may give rise to other feelings and ideas. New building does often require demolition of the old; and audacity is, after all, one form of grandeur.

Color in painting is a complex business; there is no doubt that every stroke and patch of color reflects the full consciousness and temper of the artist. All that you think about and feel goes into your eye and hand, and issues such as those discussed above, whether overtly nurtured or not, go into the occupation of being an artist and putting paint on canvas.

I do not mean to suggest that the artist should become actively concerned with questions that are really the province of art historians or theoreticians of culture.

In chapter 6, I spoke of Frankenthaler's canvas as "a metaphor for a provisional, transient universe." As an observer, I can make that assessment, but that is not to say that the artist has consciously tried to match her canvas to what we might presume are her thoughts about the world. An artist more likely, and more appropriately, thinks about other artists, and about the art tradition of which he or she feels a part.

Of course, we tend to guide ourselves by one kind of painting rather than another because it echoes our own temperament and our own sense of reality. As a practical matter, though, and as working artists, we assess traditions, modes, and individual works of art. It is from them that we take our bearings, even with regard to the general world around us.

In the end we must acknowledge that the most important things about painting cannot be said with words, that what we all know to be most important is not aided by discourse. No doubt there are times in this book when I have pushed the analysis of a painting a bit too far, have seemed to squeeze the mystery of a painting dry, and you have wanted to protest, "But what about feeling? Isn't that the most important thing?" Yes, that is the most important thing.

Still, can my purpose be fulfilled by urging you on to feel more strongly? Surely that would be useless; you don't need that. By definition, an artist is one who converts feelings into color, into paint. My *Portrait of Leo Steinberg* is an example of such conversion; it is one about which I can speak fully because I know its genesis.

For reasons of practicality and temperament, the portrait was to be done in one sitting of three hours. As is usual for me in such cases, I had prepared several canvases of appropriate size. The preparation consisted of tinting each of them slightly; experience had shown me that, given the restricted time (I work only while the sitter is present), it is sometimes necessary to leave parts of the canvas untouched, and I have found the untinted white of the primed canvas generally too harsh to be integrated with the rest of the colors. As I recall, I had tinted, with a wash of turpentine, two canvases warm (faintly peach-colored) and two cool (a very light blue).

When Steinberg arrived at my studio, my very first impression was that he had aged. I had not expected that. In the past few years, had I indeed seen him only in the dim light of the lecture hall? In the bright light of my studio, I saw that time had shadowed his eyes—the skin around them seemed strangely purple. It was the stab of mortality, and it churned in me as we greeted each other and he mounted the stand. A peach-colored canvas was out of the question; I put a blue one on the easel.

I then noticed that he was wearing a light blue shirt. A dusky red and a light blue hung in my mind, blue as base. Tentatively, I painted an extended patch of blue—the plane or facade that would carry the features.

I am laying out, with brush and with mind, the range of tones: two dull red patches, the eye sockets. The same red contours the forehead. Change colors again. I stretch with black the extent of the head from top of canvas to chin and beard. Inside me the churning has stopped. I have put down two patches of dull red, not reflecting on mortality but on the fact that even without much blue in them, those reds upon their beds of blue seem purplish while the same red as forehead contour seems brighter, warm against the paler blue. Then, I realize, I have put down blue and I have put down red; the sharp projection of the nose needs another hue and I have only yellow left. The blue and the red are not bright, but the yellow is. O.K. Still, only fifteen minutes into the painting, I have

Irving Kriesberg *Portrait of Leo Steinberg*. Oil on canvas, 1981
(34 × 28 inches). Courtesy of the artist.

70   Working With Color

staked things out more widely and more definitely than I had intended.

Chagrined and a bit buffaloed, I retreat from the head and sketch out with black the shoulders and lapels, against which the planes and angles of the head will be opposed.*

But I must tackle the face. Squinting, I view the parameters of my territory: light blue, dark red, cold yellow. And black and gray. The features must be detailed within that range of color. Some warmer colors are needed to extend, to fill in the range. A red contour has marked the outer edge of the forehead's projection; the near side I indicate with a patch of warm yellow, almost as pale as the light blue that surrounds it. But its bright warmth suggests an even brighter apricot stroke for the bridge of the nose—a color that rises out of the blue matrix and links up with the yellow peak of the nose, but whose reddishness links it also to the low lying sockets from which it rises. Almost the same light red indicates the thrust of the lower lip.

Leave the face, I tell myself. The shoulders are opposed to the head but they need to be connected by more than a light blue smudge. The tilt and bulge of the shoulder contour on the right edge of the painting suggests a bulge of darker blue—a peculiar carriage, "my horse's neck" Steinberg says of himself—and its rhythm, starting from below, rises up to meet the black vertical band that earlier, mistakenly, was meant to indicate the back contour of the head. I complete the upward stroke with a flourish of an ear, realize there is no room for it yet, and wipe it away. It never reappears. Instead a jumble of bluish gray-black is painted in to indicate the back contour.

Reminded by the false flourish that calligraphy is nevertheless part of my inspiration, I use the same color and rhythm to characterize the beard, starting with the step-form to the right of the lower lip. That shape, together with my realization that I am working essentially with red and blue (opposed by gray-black) brings in the violet strokes marking the upper cheek, lower cheek, and neck.

I am not thinking of my feelings, nor of Steinberg's mortality, nor of his

*Some of this shoulder area is cropped in the color reproduction.

character. Sure, I am excited and tense, but it is the pressure of decisions. Now as I grope for a way to indicate the eyes in the more or less shorthand manner I see I have established, I reflect that, whatever duskiness has settled on the skin around them, his eyes themselves are as intense as ever: cobalt blue, sharpened with a bit of white and thalo green, is put down just below the thin yellow-black that indicates their slant, and below the earlier slant of the eyebrows. The near eye is enlivened with a highlight and a surround of light red to sharpen its blue; the far eye, more shadowed, is touched with dark blue. Days later, looking at them, the thought occurs to me: one eye looks outward; the other, inward. So be it.

Now to build the protrusion of cheekbone out of the light blue matrix: a sharp green-blue or aqua and its opposite, red-orange; a similar red stroke on the side of the face protrudes less here among the violet tones. I use more red to detail the mouth; a green-blue recalling the pupils indicates a parting of the lips; and slight strokes of yellow and apricot indicate their thrust.

Some relief from the system of reds and blues: I bring in some pale greens to indicate a foil of shirt, and thin green and dark blue lines etch and articulate the area around the eyes.

Two and a half hours have passed. I feel a single stroke more will disturb the fragile equilibrium. I stop and Steinberg steps down. "I have given you a yellow nose," I say. Ever the fastidious scholar, he corrects me: "In the painting, the nose is yellow." "I ran out of colors too soon." "Well, the example I cite to my students regarding language is that if we assign to that bright orb in the sky the word 'sun,' we cannot assign the same word to that pale evening orb. A single word may be arbitrary, but in a system, it never is."

We did not speak of feelings then, nor have we since. I have tried here to be as specific as possible about the relation between feeling and working; to be more precise, I have described how the process of working displaces the awareness of those affects we commonly call feelings. I cannot with any authority say whether the portrait expresses a sense of mortality or my concern about it. As a working artist, I find such questions useless, even though as an observer I know that in the end those are the issues the paint must address.

10

A CODA

How important to the working artist are theoretical ideas about art? On one level they are profoundly important. It is hard to imagine how an artist could seriously proceed without an established tradition, a way of working based on accepted principles, whether or not these are consciously articulated. One such set of principles is given abbreviated expression in the commonly held idea that the business of the visual artist is to represent nature faithfully.

That idea was deliberately abandoned by certain artists early in this century and it was modified or given special meaning by others. All who did not accept it, however, substituted something in its place.

Without doubt, this has been the most prodigiously inventive century in the history of all art; hundreds and hundreds of great works have been produced in an enormous array of modes, and these have expanded our mind astonishingly.

For this reason, it would seem worthwhile to review some of the ideas that have been proclaimed during the past hundred years as the theoretical bases of new art.

When set down baldly, however, these ideas often seem outrageously irrational or simple-minded, as you will see. The only legitimate conclusion in the face of this paradox is that—regardless of how important ideas and theories and manifestos have been in fueling the production of great art—the individual temperament and genius of the artist must be of primary importance. The work of art, even though it may be the manifestation of a mental idea, is equally the manifestation of a unique individuality expressing itself in a particular format of materials; and individuality and materials seem to have their own insistent ideas—which is itself a very imposing paradox.

Consider the case of Mondrian. Among the painters discussed in our book, he is perhaps the strictest ideologue. His mystical conception of purism sought to reduce painting to its "essentials." The physical austerity of his studio reflected not so much the meagerness of his financial resources as it did the minimalism of his creed. His furnishings as well as his paintings consisted of squares of primary color.

Mondrian's power and originality as an artist is very nearly universally acknowledged, but the general soundness of his theories is another matter. He insisted that all lines in his paintings be strictly horizontal or vertical. Yet a good number of his works—the one reproduced here, for example—are presented as diamond-shaped: the diagonals of the frame and the resulting spaces provide a complex counterpoint to the vertical and horizontal elements in his painting. Moreover, by introducing black, white, and gray into his paintings in addition to the primary colors, he set up an aggregate of interactions that is far from minimal.

Indeed, the whole idea of red, yellow, and blue as primary colors is really arbitrary, not objective or scientific. Do those colors represent the three basic sensations of color as experienced by the eye? That would be hard to argue, since "basic sensations of the eye" are really culturally determined; what the eye sees is to an important extent what the mind expects it to see. Among Western painters the color wheel is a basic ideogram, but the color wheel is a chart that reproduces the spectrum of light only in a crude and arbitrary form. For a painter, the primacy of red, yellow, and blue pigments derives from the fact that, in a very rough way, many other hues may be achieved by mixing pigments of these colors while they themselves cannot be achieved by mixing pigments of other colors. Yet that fact is not based on any scientific or objective analysis of color itself but is simply manifested in our experience with paint pigments.

Photo technicians who determine the composition of the dyes that make up the layers of light-sensitive emulsion on color film and on color printing paper find, pragmatically, that another set of basic colors, including such nonpainterly designations as cyan and magenta is necessary to produce the full range of colors the eye is capable of seeing.

Similarly, printing press operators, in reproducing color images, have hit upon a red, yellow, and blue in their printing inks that are significantly different from the primary colors Mondrian used on his palette. Printers, moreover add a fourth color, black, to achieve the full range of color sensations. These determinations have been developed over years of trial and error, based on the interaction of mechanical devices involving photographic dyes, camera filters, printing inks, and patterns of halftone dots—a mixing procedure quite different from that of the painter.

Stage designers and other technicians who use electric lights to mix colors find that their "primaries" and their mixing results are very different from the painter's in a studio or the photo technician's in a lab.

Thus it seems that, while Mondrian's ideas of minimalism in color did, in his case, inspire him to achieve canvases that are quite powerful in their severity, there is little in the theory itself that has universal application or that resembles an objective analysis of color phenomena.

Expositions and arguments of this sort have not, of course, prevented artists from promulgating new manifestos based on other "universal truths." Following is a list of some of those ideas and programs. All were initially considered outlandish; many still are considered so. In my opinion, common sense would reject them all—if only their practitioners had not animated them with undeniable masterpieces.

1. The *Impressionists* believed that the artist's eye should be only an instrument for recording color sensations or impressions from nature—a narrow, mechanistic idea from which one could never have predicted the many glorious paintings created under its aegis.

2. The *Postimpressionists* (Gauguin and Van Gogh, among others) argued that the colors the artist chooses need not be natural—indeed, that they should be invented freely—even though Postimpressionists painted scenes from nature.

3. *Kandinsky* and other followers of various mystic orders claimed that the colors

they used had specific reference to entities and conditions that exist on an "astral plane," a nonmaterial world.

4. The *Cubists* systematically reduced the richness of natural objects to a fugue of simple geometric planes. Often Cubists allowed a single canvas to carry several different perceptions simultaneously.

5. The *Collagists* made whole works out of broken fragments, pieced together disjunctively. (The new art of cinema adopted this idea as its most basic and enduring language.)

6. The *Dadaists* proclaimed the value of non-sense above sense in art and culture. As artists, they were intent on creating, in their own words, anti-art.

7. The *Surrealists* valued irrationality above reason.

8. *Personal Symbolists*—Redon, Chagall, Miró, Beckmann, Jensen, and others—gained wide public acceptance, though their imagery was entirely private and nobody really claimed to read them.

9. *Neoprimitivism* is an attitude (cf. Dubuffet and others) that views not refinement, but undeveloped crudity as an artistic value to be worked toward.

10. *Conceptualists* such as Marcel Duchamp claimed that in art, the idea was more important than the object made. In true conformity to his credo, Duchamp stopped creating works of art.

11. *Prescription art* developed when artists such as Joseph Kosuth limited their role in the production of works of art to the making of descriptive charts. This idea is premised on the position that the "creating" artist (e.g. Moholy Nagy, Sol Lewitt) can appropriately confine personal creative participation to the specifying of certain models or parameters, and then allow others to execute the work.

12. *Social artists*—the Russian Constructivists, the Mexican muralists, the Americans Ben Shahn, Grant Wood, and certain contemporaries—today are honored

or ignored as individuals, and not for the social ideas they believed their art conveyed.

13. *Abstract Expressionists* or *action painters* argued that more meaningful paintings could be achieved by attacking the canvas with as little premeditation as possible.

14. *Pop art* introduced the notion that direct reproduction of popular images on traditional artistic media—for example, the literal transference of commercial images onto canvas—should be called (high) art.

15. *Bad art* is essentially an attitude that art that is ungainly, inept, in bad taste has for that reason qualities to be valued.

This list of paradoxes is not intended to discredit the modernist enterprise or even to discredit the value of ideas for the artist. For many artists, these agendas provided a serious stimulus for the creation of vigorous and enduring works. My presentation is intended only to demonstrate my thesis that no program or theory has universal prescriptive value.

The remaining paradox is this: having as an observer argued against universalist dogmas, I cannot, as an artist, argue against your embracing an idea that someone else may call hare-brained and running with it as though your life depended on it!

PART 2

WORKING PROCEDURES

11

THE STUDIO:
MATERIALS, SPACE, LIGHTING

If you are relatively new to the occupation of painting, you will save yourself a good deal of future grief by immediately adopting such studio practices as keeping your brushes clean, capping your jars and tubes promptly, and preparing and stretching your canvases properly. Your ability to call forth the precise color you want comes first of all from the clarity of your intent, but it requires also that your materials be in good working order.

Buying Materials

In shopping for materials, the general rule is that you get what you pay for. Cheaper oil paints generally contain less pigment per tube (and more filler) and therefore require more paint to do the same job of covering. A cheaper brush is usually less satisfactory in retaining its shape and in resiliency, which generally results in your using it less, thus making it no bargain at all.

Prices vary considerably in different supply stores, so you should shop around. In a large city where retail art suppliers compete with each other, prices may be lower. Quantity buying, particularly of canvas and paper, can bring the price down significantly, so you may want to join with some fellow artists in placing larger orders. If you live in a smaller town that has only one local supplier, a group of you might approach the merchant proposing larger orders for lower prices.

Studio Space and Lighting

Probably no studio space is ever large enough, whether you live in the city or in the country and whether your work is large or small. The size of your space may depend on how much rent you can pay or on how much of your home you can wrangle from your family. In my opinion a minimum-size studio will permit you to walk back far enough not only to take in the whole painting at once, but even to get a somewhat distant view. You should also be able to set up your painting in various places in your studio, so that you can see it in slightly modified ambience and light. Your studio should also be large enough to let you keep several other works out and visible.

Proper lighting is crucial. If possible, all your light should come from skylights or windows facing north; the light is steadier and devoid of shafts of sunlight that can be disconcerting as they streak and move across your walls. Of course, all of us are dependent to some extent on artificial light. The incandescent bulbs generally used in homes and workplaces—and even in galleries and museums—provide light by electrically heating a filament to incandescence. The resulting light lacks a bit of the blue we find in natural daylight, so we call it yellow. You can demonstrate the effect of this by arranging a stick to cast two shadows, one from daylight, the other from an incandescent bulb; you will notice that the shadow cast by the bulb is cool in hue, while the shadow cast by the blue daylight is warm in hue.

Some artists consider it useless to speak of daylight since their work is almost always seen under artificial light, whether in a home, a gallery, or a museum. To my mind there can be no other norm than daylight, particularly when we remember that by "natural light" we mean the fullest spectrum of colors to which the human eye is sensitive. Under common incandescent bulbs, the blue in your painting will appear slightly duller.

The light that illuminates your painting therefore needs to be daylight or a true white artificial light.

One solution is to install fluorescent fixtures and fit them with "daylight white" tubes. Initial costs are higher than for incandescent lights but electricity costs are considerably lower. Yet many people find the quality of the lighting under fluorescent tubes to be unsatisfactory. Putting aside the claim that prolonged working under fluorescent lights can be injurious to health, there is no question that fluorescent lighting lacks the sparkle and bounce of actual daylight or of lighting from incandescent bulbs. This can be somewhat offset by installing a mixture of warm white and cold white tubes. My own vote is for incandescent bulbs, installed so as to mix ordinary white with blue daylight bulbs. This combination comes closest to reproducing the full range and sparkle of outdoor light. They are best installed so that they alternate in a track above your painting wall or in clamp reflectors above your easel. A minimum installation would consist of a wide reflector with a clamp, fitted with a double socket into which is screwed one 100-watt regular frosted bulb and one 100-watt daylight frosted bulb.

If your painting area is really cramped and you do not have the space to install lights at the proper distance from and angle (15°) to the canvas, you may have recourse to bouncing the light off the ceiling and walls near the canvas. Since the throw of fluorescent light is extremely short, it is not useful in any bounced light installation. The bounced incandescent light can provide a very satisfactory diffused illumination, but be sure that the wattage is ample and that the wall you are bouncing off is truly white. Make sure also that the bulbs are located in such a way that you are not facing into the light.

Brushes

The shortest thing that can be said about brushes is get the very best you can afford and keep them clean. You are better served by a few very good brushes than a large number of fair ones, none of which really does the job. A good brush can quickly become a poor one if it is allowed to get stiff or splayed. For oil painting, most artists prefer bristle brushes, which offer the best degree of maneuverability, considering the resilience of the stretched canvas and the thickness of oil paint. If your surface is rigid, you may want a softer brush, as you would when working with watercolors. The same principles will apply when working with acrylic paints. Remember that acrylic paint dries very quickly and you must keep a bucket of water on your table to plunge the brush into immediately after use.

Oil Paint Thinners and Media

As it comes from the tube, oil paint is generally too thick and dense to be applied directly to the canvas. Turpentine, which is a tree resin, is generally mixed with the paints to thin them and make application easier. Although the authority Ralph Mayer writes that mineral spirits—these are petroleum products—are perfectly suitable for thinning oil paints, most artists I know reserve mineral spirits for cleaning purposes and use only pure spirits of turpentine as a thinner. Turpentine can be used for thinning just as it comes from the can, but many artists add other materials to their thinner to impart special qualities to their paintings. For example, stand oil may be added. This is thickened linseed oil (which is the vehicle in which pigments are ground to make oil paints); it adds body and sheen to paint that has been diluted with turpentine.

I prefer my paintings to be relatively matte, so I use a dammar and wax mixture to add body to the thinner, to hasten drying somewhat and to provide a more matte finish. Dammar, a resin, comes in large granular crystals. These can be pulverized, but need not be, before being put in a pouch of cheesecloth and suspended in a covered jar of turpentine (*not* mineral spirits). After a few hours, all the crystals will be dissolved. Into this turpentine mixture I then add shavings of beeswax, which can take a day or two to dissolve completely. For every quart of turpentine, I use two heaping tablespoons of the unpulverized crystals and the same amount of wax shavings. As you use up the medium, you can add more turpentine if you wish. Too much wax can weaken the capacity of the oil paint to dry to the hard film that gives the painting its permanence.

Any material added either to the oil paint or to turpentine, its natural thinner, as a means of altering their qualities involves some risk to the permanence of the painted surface. Two recently developed products, however, have received good reports from artists: Liquin and RapidSet. Both are mixed with the oil paint (and thinned with turpentine) to hasten drying and to give greater flow to the stroke with less dripping or drag. MAGNA is a line of colors developed by Leonard Bocour; though acrylic-based, these paints may be mixed with oils or turpentine.

Keeping Brushes Clean

Oil brushes can be cleaned using mineral spirits under various trade names such as Varnolene, turpentine substitute, or paint thinner. These petroleum products are cheaper than turpentine. I do not advise using them as a painting medium or thinner, but if you do, make sure that the container you use for cleaning brushes is not the one into which you dip your brush before mixing a color. Your medium, kept in a separate container, should always be clean.

To facilitate brush cleaning, I strongly recommend the following: in an old coffee can, insert a screen so it stands about half-way down in the can. I use a ¼″ flat mesh which I cut and shape to fit. Any ready-made device that can act as a strainer will do. Fill the can about three-quarters full with paint thinner. To clean your brush simply immerse it in the cleaner and work it against the strainer. The sediment will go to the bottom and once every few months you can fish out the strainer and remove the sludge or just throw the whole thing out and start again. Brushes can be kept working clean this way. It is not really necessary to wash them with soap and water every evening. A few times a year, or whenever your brushes become too stiff you can use a soak of trisodium phosphate. Dissolve a few tablespoons of powdered trisodium phosphate in half a coffee can of water, soak for several hours or overnight, and rinse thoroughly with water;* if you like a nicely shaped brush, wrap the hairs in a bit of newspaper and let them dry inside that little packet.

*As trisodium phosphate is a potential water pollutant, it should be disposed of as garbage and not simply poured down the drain.

Always have plenty of clean paint cloths around. They are indispensable for wiping your brush before and after the mesh treatment. They are also good for maintaining a clear surface on your palette and for removing fresh oil paint from your canvas when you are making major changes and don't want to wait. If the paint is really thick on your canvas, you first may have to remove all you can with a palette knife. That, by the way, is the only use I have for the palette knife. To use the knife to mix large quantities of a single color or to apply paint to the canvas is to nullify the most positive aspect of oil painting: its receptivity to the most complex and subtle mixing of colors. For mixing paint on the palette and spreading it on the canvas, the brush is an infinitely richer tool than the knife.

Acrylic Paint

Modern acrylic artists' colors have all the body and intensity of oil paints. Being a fast-drying medium, however, acrylic must be handled very differently. Acrylic can be handled in a wide range of techniques. Diluted with water it can be worked quite thin, like the most delicate transparent watercolor. Acrylic, unlike linseed oil, does not eat the fibers of cotton or linen cloth and therefore can be applied on the raw, ungessoed canvas. Artists such as Jackson Pollock, Morris Louis, and Helen Frankenthaler took advantage of that characteristic to develop techniques for dripping and pouring acrylic paint directly onto the raw canvas.

The most characteristic use of acrylic paint is to cover large flat surfaces, mixing the colors first in jars. An artist who decides to alter one of the areas simply mixes a new jar of color and repaints that surface. Using masking tape, the artist can achieve extremely straight, clean edges and even narrow straight lines.

Acrylic paint can also be used in modes similar to oil paint, including working wet on wet and building impasto. However, the latter mode requires mixing the paint with retarders and thickeners to slow the drying and give the paint the necessary bulk for impasto. Various procedures can be developed to keep the acrylic from drying while you work. The paint can be sprayed with water or retarder on the palette, and even, if you are careful, on the canvas. Colors can be squeezed out of tubes onto a palette and covered with Saranwrap or squeezed into palettes shaped with concavities that are half-filled with water. Many artists work acrylic in ways that are virtually identical with oils. One general advantage of acrylic over oil is that, being fast drying, it allows you to make radical changes in the painting without the risk of building up thick paint into an unworkable sludge.

To the never-ending controversy over the comparative virtues of acrylic versus oil, I can only offer this anecdote—the end of a joust with Al Held, a staunch and splendid practioner of flat, hard-edged acrylic: "But finally," I said, "the reason I like oil paint is because it's not hard, because it's resonant . . ." "Resonant!" he snorted, "Hell! You mean sentimental; that's what oil paint is!"

12

THE PALETTE: SELECTING COLORS

The word "palette" refers first of all to the flat piece of wood or other surface upon which you spread your bits of color. It is also, however, the range of color that you elect to lay out on that surface; and even more to the point, it is the *particular* color range, the scope within which your painting will be created. The palette is, after all, the material source of your work; your painting can come only out of that selection of colors: there is no other source. When you visit an artist's studio, you can see that there is a very direct relationship between the palette or working table, and the canvases: they are, in a material sense, mirrors of each other.

When we say a certain artist has a particular palette, we mean not only that the canvases show a recognizable color tonality, but that the work table—the colors the artist lays out—will also have that particular, recognizable character. In the end, an artist's palette reflects the artist's own temperament; in defending a particular palette, one artist's common sense is another's senseless prejudice.

Nevertheless, I am prepared to lay down some principles by which I feel the inexperienced painter ought to be guided until he or she develops modifications and displacements that accord with his or her own tested temperament.

My first principle—and perhaps the only one—is that the colors on your palette need to be the brightest, absolutely the most intense you can find. This principle is based on the simple fact that you can always modify a color; that is, you can always make it milder or grayer. In contrast, you cannot, materially speaking, produce on your canvas a red that is brighter than the brightest red on your palette. The corollary of this principle is that you do not need to put on your palette any color that you can mix. Do not buy a tube of paint that consists of a mixture from two other tubes. Your palette needs to hold essential colors, not secondary colors; this is not a matter of economy but of fundamental painting practices, about which I will have more to say later on.

Before I actually name the colors I recommend—that is, before I describe my own palette—I must inform you of the sad fact that one manufacturer's cadmium red medium may be another manufacturer's cadmium red scarlet. One manufacturer's cobalt blue may not exactly match another's, even though their designation may be the same. If you are buying a brand with which you are unfamiliar, unscrew the cap and look inside; at the very least consult a color chart provided by the manufacturer. I will use the nomenclature of Winsor-Newton oil colors; it is one of the better brands widely available in the United States. In any case, small shifts in name and in actual color do not undermine the principle I am talking about.

The first color I lay out is white; I use TITANIUM WHITE because it has very good covering and mixing power, even though it lacks the transparency and sparkle of ZINC WHITE, which some artists prefer.

To the left of that I place what will be the lightest bright color on my palette: CADMIUM YELLOW LEMON. This is a yellow that is cold and light, but quite intense: it cannot be duplicated by mixing white and green with a deeper yellow.

The next color, proceeding in the direction of a rough spectrum, is CADMIUM YELLOW PALE. This is a cool yellow—mellow but bright.

The next is CADMIUM YELLOW MEDIUM. This is a robust, rich, warm yellow, close to most people's notion of "pure" yellow.

The next is CADMIUM YELLOW DEEP. This is an orange-yellow—bright pumpkin. You cannot quite achieve its brightness by mixing cadmium yellow with cadmium red.

Next is CADMIUM RED PALE, or LIGHT, or, as Winsor-Newton

says, SCARLET. This is a very bright orange-red that is cheery and not very resonant; you cannot achieve its lightness and brightness by mixing yellow with a deeper red.

Next is CADMIUM RED MEDIUM. Some manufacturers produce a CADMIUM RED MEDIUM (SCARLET), which I recommend because it comes closest to what most of us would call a true red—full-bodied and intense. More normally, cadmium red medium is a bit heavier and darker than the "true" chromatic red we imagine.

For a darker red still, one that is very basso but still intense, I like a CADMIUM RED DEEP. Again, it is a color you cannot get by mixing, for if you add any color to cadmium red medium in order to darken it, you will also dull it.

The cadmium pigments yield this wide range of more or less evenly spaced yellows and reds. The colors are intense and have good covering and mixing power. HANSA YELLOWS and CHROME YELLOWS generally cover less well and, to my mind, do not offer anything the cadmiums cannot provide.

On the other side of white, I begin another row of colors on my palette. Although these continue the spectrum, they appear quite dark when laid out.

The first is PTHALOCYANINE GREEN (WINSOR GREEN, if you use that brand). The THALO colors, relative newcomers to the artist's palette, are extremely intense, and a little goes a long way. THALO GREEN is a dark, bluish green. When mixed with white, it creates an aqua that is almost blue; when mixed with the several cadmium yellows, it produces greens from light apple to deepest olive. Many artists like VIRIDIAN or GUIGNET'S GREEN, which is also dark and bluish, but I find that it lacks the power and brilliance (as well as the brashness) of thalo.

All other greens should be banished from your palette. Avoid especially HOOKERS GREEN, BOTTLE GREEN, SAP GREEN, TERRE VERTE. These are all dull, weak colors that will help you achieve nothing but mud.

My next color is COBALT BLUE, preferably deep. This is a "true" blue—intense in hue, but without quite as much power as I would wish.

Next is ULTRAMARINE BLUE—a blue that is somewhat darker, somewhat more purplish, with even less power than the cobalt, but quite intense when managed correctly.

I do not use any other blues. The effects of THALO BLUE, of MANGANESE BLUE, and of CERULEAN BLUE, I feel, can substantially be produced with colors I have already named.

Purples and violets are not easy colors to designate. Each manufacturer seems to offer his own range of hues and names, and each color seems to offer some advantages and some drawbacks. An old favorite is ALIZARIN CRIMSON, which is more wine-red than violet. It is very intense but has little power. Indeed, it is a transparent color and mixes unpleasantly with other colors unless you add some white. Winsor-Newton makes PERMANENT MAUVE, which is a heavy purple, somewhat bluish, somewhat transparent, and difficult to maintain as true chromatic violet. Winsor-Newton also makes PERMANENT MAGENTA, which is a somewhat reddish violet and has fairly good covering power. MANGANESE VIOLET is a purple, neither too red nor too blue, that sustains itself well in mixing.

That completes the spectrum colors, and I don't allow much else on my palette.

Of course there is BLACK, IVORY BLACK, or MARS BLACK. It is a necessary, useful color, and its hue cannot be achieved by any admixture of other colors. Some teachers instruct their students to eliminate black from their palettes because many inexperienced artists use black somewhat indiscriminately to darken colors when better ways are at hand to achieve a dark color. But black, as a color in itself, has a particular character that belongs in the painter's arsenal. Try mixing black with a bit of yellow, or black with a bit of white, or add to black a bit of blue mixed with the white or a bit of red mixed with the white, and you will see how many different blacks you can create starting with pure black from the tube.

All browns and all earth colors (siennas, umbers, and ochres) can generally be achieved with the colors I have already laid out. I do usually include YELLOW OCHRE on my palette, mostly for economy's sake. It can be achieved by dulling cadmium yellow, but in quantity that can prove a much more expensive route; achieving the darker earth colors requires a smaller investment of cadmium. Earth colors or browns are "secondary" colors, and I don't want them on my palette.

Besides the issue of hue, other qualities must be considered in choosing the colors for your palette. First, there is the question of permanence. No artist wants colors to fade or alter after some years on the canvas. Most manufacturers make very few such fugitive colors, and I will say no more about it except that you need to ascertain this if you are considering buying a particular color for the first time.

Another important consideration is the relative transparency or opaqueness of a pigment. Sometimes opaqueness is equated with strength or covering power, although it is not quite the same thing. In any case, such qualities are assessed by testing the colors for their reaction to being combined with white. For example, Alizarin crimson quickly yields its rich darkness and with only a small amount of white becomes a very light pink. Thalo Green, on the other hand, holds its potency even with a substantial admixture of white. Cadmium red light loses its yellowish glow when mixed with white, and many colors in the violet range lose their identity with only a small amount of white.

You can test these qualities on your palette in your studio. If you are in a shop, considering a new color for the first time, consult the color chart put out by the manufacturer; it usually shows the color at full strength and also cut with white. Failing that, open the tube, and thin out a bit of the paint on your finger. (If you encounter loose oil when you remove the cap, choose a different brand.) It is important of course to become familiar with the interaction of each pigment with each of the others, but white is by far the most common modifier, so its action is the most important. Your dark colors, for example, are usually too dark as they come from the tube for their particular hues to be easily distinguishable. Some admixture of white is generally necessary to give a dark color its full vitality.

My primary reason for thinking that you ought not clutter your palette with secondary colors—with colors you can mix out of the basic pigments—is that a sparer palette encourages you to use colors more analytically. If, for example, you want to put down a brown area on your canvas, and rather than plopping your brush into the ready-mixed brown, you mix your color by combining red, yellow, and black, you will automatically be making a decision as to whether the brown tends toward yellow, red, or black—whether it is to be relatively pale or relatively resonant—and this judgment in turn will be affected by consideration of the particular location and function of that brown in your painting. As you are mixing, therefore, you are saying to yourself, "I want this particular brown to have a rosy cast and to look fresh against that heavy green to the left."

I don't mean that you should be able to name every color that appears on your canvas. Some of the most joyous moments in a painting occur when the particular thickness or thinness of the paint, the scumble or sweep or piling up of a particular hue in a particular part of the canvas has an ineffable rightness that is impossible to predict and hardly possible to describe, even while you look at it. But such magic will occur only when the eye of the artist is analytic. The eye may be unconscious or intuitive, but somewhere there is an awareness of movement from warm to cool, from bright to dull, from repetition to change, from quiet to noisy.

The particular color you need at any moment in your canvas almost never exists raw from the tube. Inevitably, you must tone it to your particular need. Therefore you must know quite precisely that you are warming it or cooling it or dulling it, that you are giving it more bite or less harshness, that you are successfully changing it in some slight way to create a more precise opposition to a color already on your canvas. You modify and tone each spot of color on your canvas so that it performs a particular function. It is rare that you should need to mix more than three colors together to get the color you want. If you do mix more than three, you begin to cancel colors out, and you risk the danger of turning your color into mud.

A muddy color is not the same as a dull color. I call a color "mud" when it is lifeless, when it fails to play an active role in the total canvas. A muddy color often results from too much mixing on the palette, but the true cause is the artist's uncertainty: not being sure of the particular color to be achieved, the artist hedges and modifies, ending up with a color that goes nowhere. A final caution: avoid mud, yes; but avoid chaff, too. Some artists, also uncertain of what they want a color to do in their paintings, turn by temperament to chaff colors—bright brash hues that also go nowhere.

INDEX

Kriesberg, Irving, *52, 53*

Lewitt, Sol, 76
lighting, 82–83
Louis, Morris, 86

Malcolm, 38, 39, 52
Man with Crossed Arms, 44, *45*
Matisse, Henri, 28, 30, 34, 35, *55*, 58
Matthiasdottir, Louisa, 15, 23, 35, 58, 66, 67
Mayer, Ralph, 84
mineral spirits, 84
Miro, Joan, 57, 76
modern theories and schools of art, 73–77
Mondrian, Piet, 13, 14, 15, 20, 28, 67, 74, 75
Monet, Claude, 15, 34, 38, 54, 55, 56, 58, 61
movement, 27–32
muddy color, 93–94
Murray, Elizabeth, 24, *25, 55, 60*

Nagy, Moholy, 76

oil paints, 89–92
oil paint thinners and media, 84–85
Open Window, Nice, 15, *39*, 65
opposition, 23, 25

paint application, 58, 60
paint mixing, 18, 19, 75
paint thinning, 84–85
palette, 88–94
paradox of dimension and density, 23
Parisians Enjoying the Parc Monceau, 15, *17*
perspective, 29
Picasso, Pablo, 15, 23, 55
Pollock, Jackson, 60, 86
Portrait of Leo Steinberg, 47, *55, 71*
primary colors, 74–75
principles of color, 7–8, 10

Redon, Odilon, 76
Rosenberg, Harold, 31, 49
Rothko, Mark, 60
Royal British Academy, 8

scale, 33–36
selecting colors, 88–94
Shahn, Ben, 76
signification, 64–72
Steinberg, Leo, 47, 69, 71, 72
Stella, Frank, 14, 27, 38, 48, 49, 55, 56, 58, 60, 67
Still Life with Cheese and Pepper, 15, 35
structure, 30, 51–57
Studio, The, 15, 23, 55
studio space and lighting, 82–83
subordination, 54
substantiality, 58

Tahkt-I-Sulayman Variation 1, 14, 27, 38, 55, 67
temperament, 58–63
tension, 20–26
tinting canvases, 69
tonality, 37–41
Turner, J. M. W., 8
turpentine, 84–85

Untitled, 1980, 37, 42

Van Gogh, Vincent, 75
variation, 55
Victory Boogie Woogie, 13, 14, 20, *22*

warm and cool, 44
wax, 84
white light, 82
Wood, Grant, 76

Yale Graduate School of Art, 67